HIDDEN TREASURES

*Traveling the Back Roads of the
Bible in Search of Truth*

Judson Edwards

Smyth & Helwys Publishing, Inc.
6316 Peake Road
Macon, Georgia 31210-3960
1-800-747-3016
©2007 by Smyth & Helwys Publishing
All rights reserved.
Printed in the United States of America.

The paper used in this publication meets the minimum requirements of
American National Standard for Information Sciences—
Permanence of Paper for Printed Library Materials.
ANSI Z39.48–1984. (alk. paper)

Library of Congress Cataloging-in-Publication Data

Edwards, Judson.
Hidden Treasures : Traveling the Back Roads of the Bible
by Judson Edwards.
p. cm.
ISBN 978-1-57312-483-6 (pbk. : alk. paper)
1. Bible–Meditations.
I. Title.
BS491.5.E39 2007
220.6—dc22

2006038944

Contents

INTRODUCTION

More than twenty years ago, a writer named William Least Heat-Moon wrote a bestselling book titled *Blue Highways*. The book was a chronicle of his 13,000-mile journey across America. When he embarked on that journey, he was determined to stay on the "blue highways," the roads marked in blue on his map. The major thoroughfares and big freeways were printed in red, but the back roads were in blue, and that's where William Least Heat-Moon wanted to be.

He wanted to meander the country roads and quiet lanes dotted with drug stores, fruit stands, and drive-in movies. He thought he could get in touch with the real America if he stayed on the blue highways.

I thought about calling this book *Blue Highways of the Bible* but eventually decided against it. That title does capture, though, what I'm trying to do in the pages that follow. I want to roam the blue highways of Scripture and look for hidden treasures on the back roads of the Bible.

Anyone familiar with the Bible knows the "red-highway" passages, the parts known and revered by the masses: the Ten Commandments, the 23rd Psalm, the Sermon on the Mount, the parable of the prodigal son, and the apostle Paul's description of love in 1 Corinthians 13, to mention a few. Those are wonderful roads to travel, full of pleasure and insight, and I'm glad I've been there.

But in these pages I want us to take the roads less traveled. I want us to get off the beaten path, meet unfamiliar people, and visit unusual places. You probably know Peter, James, and John, but in these pages I want you to meet Bezalel, Ahimaaz, and Diotrephes. And you've probably spent some time studying Matthew, Mark, Luke, and John, but I want you to visit Lamentations, Habakkuk, Haggai, and 3 John. Even if you've spent a good part of your life studying the Bible, we'll probably go places you've seldom been before.

As we wander the back roads of the Bible, I think you'll be impressed with the people we meet and the sights we see. You might even come to believe there are truths to be learned on the back roads that can't be learned anywhere else.

The chapters in this book are short for two reasons. First, I like short chapters and think they make a book readable. Second, I've opted for short chapters because of what I'm trying to do in the book. My goal is to whet your appetite, to give you just enough to make you want to go to the Bible and explore these passages in more depth. There is nothing exhaustive in any of these chapters, but I hope there *is* something tantalizing.

The chapters are in order of the biblical books they discuss. The first chapter deals with a passage from Genesis, and the last chapter deals with a passage from Revelation. In between, the chapters move through the Old and New Testaments, dealing with some books and ignoring others. There are hidden treasures in every book of the Bible, but space constraints compelled me to pick and choose.

Because the chapters move in order through the Bible, there's no topical, thematic organization to the book. One chapter might deal with grace, and the next one might ricochet over to suffering. If it feels a bit disjointed, forgive me. It could be that the best way to approach this book is to read a chapter, ponder the questions for reflection that go with it, let the truth of that chapter sink in, and then move on to the next one. My guess is that a slow reading of the book will be more rewarding than a fast one. The book conveniently has thirty-one chapters, at least one for each day of the month.

I'm writing this book while on a sabbatical at a cabin in Oregon. Every morning I get to wake up, pour myself a cup of coffee, and then head to the computer to explore the blue highways of the Bible. I'm going to have a lot of fun on this journey, and I hope you will too.

Each morning as I write, I'm going to visualize the people I'm writing for:

- Christians who have been in church all their lives and know all about the Bible but long for something fresh.
- Preachers and Bible teachers needing a new word to declare to their listeners.
- People who like to explore out-of-the-way places in search of adventure.

If you're in one of those three categories, I invite you to come along and wander the blue highways with me. I'm hoping we'll find some hidden treasures along the way.

1

PLAN B

The matter distressed Abraham greatly because it concerned his son. But God said to him, "Do not be so distressed about the boy and your maidservant. . . . I will make the son of the maidservant into a nation also, because he is your offspring." (Genesis 21:11-13)

The Christopher Reeve story captivated America. He was a handsome young actor best known for playing Superman in the movies. But his life changed forever on May 17, 1995, at a horse show in Virginia. The horse Christopher Reeve was riding balked and stopped short at a jump, and Reeve, his hands tangled in the bridle, catapulted headfirst onto the ground. The accident left him a quadriplegic, confined to a ventilator and a wheelchair.

Until he died on October 10, 2004, Christopher Reeve lived with a tenacious courage that inspired people around the world. But the irony in his story was easy to see: Even Superman suffered. And even Superman had to have a Plan B.

The first hidden treasure I want you to notice concerns Abraham, one of the great heroes of the Bible and a character known to anyone familiar with Scripture. We know the plot of his story well. What we *don't* always notice is that Abraham had to cope with a Plan B of his own.

Abraham's story can be plotted like points on a graph:

> • Abraham gets called by God to leave Haran and go to the land of
> Canaan. God promises to bless him, make his name great, and
> number his descendants as many as the stars.
> • Even in his old age, Abraham is promised a son by God and, sure
> enough, a son is born to him. It is such a delightful, surprising event
> that Abraham and his wife, Sarah, name the boy Isaac, which means
> "laughter."
> • Abraham proves his faith in God by being willing to sacrifice this
> special son to God, but God spares the boy. Abraham's place in his-
> tory as a great man of faith is secure, though, and, as we will see in
> the next chapter, he is consistently held up in the Bible as one of the
> "superstars" of faith.

That storyline is well known—Abraham, Sarah, and Isaac following
God, being faithful to God, living out the blessing of God. What is
not so well known is the subplot in the Abraham story. If the main
plot of the story is marked by laughter, the subplot of the story is
marked by tears.

The subplot goes something like this: Abraham and Sarah move to
Canaan, but they don't have a son. They live in Canaan ten long years
and still no son is born. Sarah, in desperation, proposes another plan:
"The Lord has kept me from having children. Go, sleep with my
maidservant; perhaps I can build a family through her" (Gen 16:2).
Abraham does precisely that, and a son, Ishmael, is born by this maidservant, Hagar. Tragically, things don't go well at all. The story
becomes one of jealousy, rage, and bad blood between Sarah and
Hagar. It becomes dark and embarrassing, the sort of drama you
might see on your favorite soap opera.

It reaches its climax in Genesis 21 when Sarah declares that Hagar
and Ishmael have to leave. She has now given birth to her beloved son,
Isaac, so Hagar and Ishmael are no longer needed to assure that
Abraham's descendants will number as many the stars. They're expend-
able now, and Sarah sends them packing.

Poor Abraham is caught squarely in the middle of a major domes-
tic dispute: "The matter distressed Abraham greatly because it

concerned his son" (Gen 21:11). He begrudgingly accedes to Sarah's wishes, though, and Hagar and Ishmael are banished to the desert of Beersheba. They're hot, thirsty, miserable, and bound for sure disaster. Things don't look good at all for this sad duo, trudging alone through the desert.

Surprisingly, though, the story takes a positive turn. God enters the picture, and everything changes in a heartbeat: "God heard the boy crying, and the angel of God called to Hagar from heaven and said to her, 'What is the matter, Hagar? Do not be afraid; God has heard the boy crying as he lies there. Lift the boy up and take him by the hand, for I will make him into a great nation'" (Gen 21:17-18).

God opens Hagar's eyes, and she sees a well of water. She drinks and gives Ishmael a drink. The future looks more promising for the two of them. By the time the curtain closes on the story, you know they're going to make it after all: "God was with the boy as he grew up. He lived in the desert and became an archer. While he was living in the Desert of Paran, his mother got a wife for him from Egypt" (Gen 21:20-21).

Here's the wonderful thing about the entire Abraham story in Genesis: Both the main plot and the subplot get blessed by God. Plan A—the Abraham, Sarah, Isaac plot—gets God's blessing. But Plan B—the Abraham, Hagar, Ishmael subplot—gets God's blessing too.

It's a good story to read, not only because it's as entertaining as a soap opera, but also because it reminds us that God can bless Plan B's. That's an encouraging reminder because most of us are now moving full-speed ahead in some Plan B of our own.

We each started out with a clear, if unspoken, Plan A. We had our dreams and goals in mind and were confident of the way life would unfold. We would fall madly in love with the perfect person and have a long and loving marriage. We would go to college, perhaps, and graduate with honors. We would have a couple of perfect children who would never give us a moment's trouble. We would chase a dream—playing shortstop for the New York Yankees, becoming a professional golfer, owning our own floral business, living in a Swiss chalet—and succeed magnificently. We would be healthy, wealthy, and wise all of our days and die at an old age with a smile on our face.

We were sure that's the way it would go, but something unexpected happened somewhere along the way to Plan A. What happened was *life*, with all of its complex, crazy twists and turns. Someone we loved more than anyone in the world had the audacity to get sick and die. Or the marriage made in heaven turned out to be hellish. Or the kids turned out to be a constant source of grief. Or the dream died in a heap of unpaid bills. Or the notion of being healthy, wealthy, and wise went down in a flame of pain, poverty, and stupidity.

We're not exactly sure how it happened, but we know it to be a fact: Plan A has officially unraveled, and we are now deeply mired in Plan B. The road to the good life has taken an irrevocable detour, and we are bound for territory we never thought we'd be exploring. Some days we wake up and wonder how we ever got in this mess and, more importantly, how we're ever going to get out of it.

It is, for most of us, the central question of life: What am I going to do with Plan B? When you think about it, our options are actually pretty simple.

We can choose to give up, throw in the towel, and grow bitter and depressed. We can declare ourselves a colossal failure and spend the rest of our days at a personal pity party. I know people who have chosen this option, and I can understand how easy it would be to go there.

Or we can choose to believe that something like this strange subplot in the Abraham story in Genesis can happen to us. We can choose to believe that God can take our embarrassing failures and flaws and bless them. We can dare to say that our own Hagars and Ishmaels might be a part of God's plan for us, and that God can take this unholy mix of divorce, death, disaster, and deception and make something holy of it. Sure, it seems unlikely, but it must have seemed unlikely to Abraham too.

When God enters the picture, everything changes. It all changes because God brings grace to the situation, and grace makes all things new.

In his book *How Can It Be All Right When Everything Is All Wrong?* Lewis Smedes writes of a time when he was nearly overcome by his Plan B:

I had never known such lonely pain, never such fear, never such helplessness, never such despair. I was utterly lost. I felt a life of pious trying going down the drain, a life of half-baked belief in grace exposed as futile. I was sunk. I screamed for help, and none could come. I was making my bed in hell. . . . I discovered, all by myself, in touch only with my final outpost of feeling, that I could be left, deserted, alone, all my scaffolds knocked down, all the stanchions beneath me pulled away, my buttresses fallen, I could be stripped of human hands, and I could survive. In my deepest heart I survived, stood up, stayed whole, held by nothing at all except the grace of a loving God.[1]

When we think of grace, we don't usually think of the Old Testament. We think of the New Testament with its message of the cross, forgiveness, and freedom. But grace is at the heart of the Abraham story in Genesis. God gave Abraham far more than he deserved, and you see it clearly in his Plan B. Abraham learned what Lewis Smedes learned: he could survive, and even thrive, held by nothing at all except the grace of a loving God.

Add up the main characters in the main plot of the Abraham story—Abraham, Sarah, and Isaac—and you expect to come up with blessing.

But add up the main characters in the subplot of the story—Abraham, Hagar, and Ishmael—and you expect to come up with disaster. It is only the incredible grace of God that could make the sure disaster into the surprising blessing it became.

Many people believe the current Arab-Israeli conflict has its roots in this Isaac-Ishmael story. They trace the Jews back to Isaac and the Arabs to Ishmael and say the two have been at odds ever since Genesis days. Even if that is true, though, it only underscores the sad tendency we humans have to sabotage God's will. The Genesis story makes it plain that God wanted to bless both Isaac and Ishmael. Whatever fighting has taken place through the centuries by their descendants has been in opposition to God's will, not because of it. God's desire was to bless Plan A *and* Plan B.

When the writer of Genesis tells us about the death of Abraham, he says, "His sons Isaac and Ishmael buried him in the cave of

Machpelah" (Gen 25:9). The two sons together burying their father. Plan A and Plan B, side by side, saying goodbye. Both grieving, and both blessed.

Only grace could make that happen.

Note

[1] Lewis Smedes, *How Can It Be All Right When Everything Is All Wrong?* (San Francisco: Harper & Row, 1982), 115.

For Reflection and Discussion

1. Even though Sarah suggested the Plan B to Abraham, she was upset when it became a reality. Why?

2. Why do you think Abraham was willing to banish Hagar and Ishmael to Beersheba?

3. Is there a difference between *our* Plan A and *God's* Plan A for our lives?

4. Can you think of other biblical characters whose Plan B was blessed by God?

5. What has happened in your life to move you to Plan B? Has God blessed your Plan B? Do you think the blessing will come?

THE GOD OF ABRAHAM, ISAAC, AND JACOB

"Do not come any closer," God said. "Take off your sandals, for the place where you are standing is holy ground." Then he said, "I am the God of your father, the God of Abraham, Isaac, and Jacob." At this Moses hid his face, because he was afraid to look at God. (Exodus 3:5-6)

"The God of Abraham, Isaac, and Jacob" is a familiar phrase to most of us. It pops up in Scripture from time to time, and it probably doesn't seem like a hidden treasure at all. But I'm guessing that most of us have never really thought about that description of God and the theological truth it contains. It's a hidden treasure not because we've never heard it but because we've never *pondered* it.

When the phrase "the God of Abraham, Isaac, and Jacob" appears in the Bible, it is used to connect God to history. It's the way the biblical writers reminded their readers that the God they wrote about is the same God who was revealed to Abraham, Isaac, and Jacob.

When Simon Peter, for example, tells a crowd of onlookers in Acts 3 that "the God of Abraham, Isaac, and Jacob, the God of our fathers, has glorified Jesus," he is telling them this is not a new God involved in the cross and resurrection but the same God who had already worked through their Jewish forefathers.

"The God of Abraham, Isaac, and Jacob" is primarily a historical reference, then, reminding people that God has a history and that God has done specific things in the past.

What we often fail to notice, though, is that "the God of Abraham, Isaac, and Jacob" also has *theological* implications and that it teaches us some profound truths about the character of God. We blithely declare God to be "the God of Abraham, Isaac, and Jacob" without stopping to consider the theological implications of that phrase.

Abraham, Isaac, and Jacob were three very different men. Though they represent three generations in the same family, they had little in common. But God was the God of each of them, and that's where the hidden treasure starts to surface.

Abraham was a *superstar*. He has always been considered one of the great characters of faith in the Bible. God chose him to be the father of the Hebrew people, and Abraham validated that choice by exhibiting a persistent trust and a dogged obedience.

At the call of God, he was willing to pull up roots and move his family from the comfort of Haran to a life of uncertainty in Canaan. He was willing to sacrifice his beloved son, Isaac, as a symbol of his allegiance to God. As we saw in the previous chapter, he was also willing to let God bless his Plan B with Hagar and Ishmael. It's not surprising that when the writer of the book of Hebrews mentions the heroes and heroines of faith in Hebrews 11, Abraham gets more notice than anyone else. In the eyes of the writer of Hebrews, Abraham was definitely one of the superstars of faith.

Call it what you will—faith, obedience, commitment, motivation—some people have it in spades. When that quality is hitched to opportunity, a superstar is born. These unusual people step out of the shadows to demand our attention and show us what real faith looks like.

When we start to assign people to the faith hall of fame, it's easy to pick some of the superstars. Abraham, Moses, David, Isaiah, Jeremiah, and Daniel get elected on the first ballot. Peter, James, and John get elected too, as do Paul, Timothy, and Barnabas. Lest we be accused of gender bias, we need to put Rahab, Ruth, and Mary on our list as well.

When we move beyond the pages of Scripture, other candidates step forward and make for easy choices: Augustine, Luther, Calvin, Spurgeon, Moody, Booth, Fosdick, Clarence Jordan, and Mother Teresa. These people, and others, have become well-known models of faith, and we are grateful for their witness.

But many of us will never be on that list. Maybe our resolve is not as strong as the resolve of those superstars. Maybe our mind is not as sharp, our personality as dynamic, or our opportunity as apparent. For whatever reason, we're not expecting to go down in history as a faith hall-of-famer.

We definitely appreciate those superstars, though, and are inspired by the trails they have blazed for us. Suffice it to say that Abraham belongs at the top of the list as one of the superstars of faith, so it's not surprising that God would be "the God of Abraham."

Isaac, however, is another matter. If Abraham could be called a superstar, Isaac could be dubbed a *nobody*. That might be putting it a little strongly, but Isaac has never made the hall of fame and never will.

We actually know little about Isaac. He is best remembered as Abraham's son and Jacob's father. Beyond that, we don't know much. We do know that Abraham was willing to sacrifice him on the altar when he was a boy. We do know that his son, Jacob, hoodwinked him when Isaac was an old man and giving out the family blessing. That's about all we know about Isaac. He's a rather obscure figure in the Bible.

I guess, for that reason, we have an easier time identifying with Isaac than with Abraham. Isaac is "every man" and "every woman." He symbolizes all of us *nobodies* who will never make headlines, blaze trails, or populate halls of fame.

I have reluctantly concluded that I might spend my whole life in an Isaac-like, flying-under-the-radar fashion. It's entirely possible that I will never preach to as many people or make as big an impact on the world as Billy Graham. It's also possible that my book sales will never match John Grisham's. I'm about to decide that my tennis game will never climb to the level of a Roger Federer and that I will never be an Eric Clapton on the guitar. I might not exactly be a nobody, but I'm not exactly a superstar either. I've settled into a nice groove of anonymity.

So, the good news for a person like me is that God is "the God of Isaac." God doesn't embrace just the *superstar* Abrahams of the world; the *nobody* Isaacs of the world get embraced too.

The big surprise, though, is that God is also "the God of Jacob." To put it bluntly, Jacob was a *scoundrel.* He cheated his brother Esau on two occasions, tricked Isaac into giving him the family blessing, and became a wealthy man by double-crossing his father-in-law, Laban. It seems that every time we meet Jacob in the book of Genesis, he's trying to con someone.

But one day Jacob had an experience that changed his life. He wrestled with a mysterious angel of God and had his name changed during the tussle. He became "Israel," gave up his conniving ways, and was a new man. That God would even pursue a scoundrel like Jacob and want to bless him is a shocking idea.

But Jacob's experience is actually the rule, not the exception, in the Bible. In Scripture, God consistently chooses people not *because of* but *in spite of.*

God chose Moses *in spite of* the fact that he had killed a man.

God chose Rahab *in spite of* her work as a harlot.

God chose Ruth *in spite of* the fact that she wasn't a Jew.

God chose David *in spite of* the fact that he was a simple shepherd boy.

God chose Saul of Tarsus *in spite of* his persecution of Christians.

God chose Simon Peter *in spite of* his volatile temperament.

Throughout the Bible, God proves to be the God of Abraham, Isaac, and, wonder of wonders, that "con man" Jacob.

When we think about the character of God, we tend to wax theological and start spouting long words. We talk about God being omniscient, omnipresent, and omnipotent. I believe God is all of those "omnis," but they don't stir me nearly as much as this simple biblical phrase we tend to skim over and never ponder. God is "the God of Abraham, Isaac, and Jacob."

God welcomes the *superstars*, the *nobodies*, and the *scoundrels*. Whosoever will may come. The only prerequisite is the willingness to be used.

For Reflection and Discussion

1. With which of these three men do you most identify? Why?

2. Who are your modern-day heroes or heroines of faith? Why do you see them as superstars?

3. Who has been the most influential in your own life—superstars, nobodies, or scoundrels?

4. Can you think of scoundrels, other than Jacob, God called and used?

5. *Fill in the blank*: God chose me in spite of _____.

THE WORK OF OUR HANDS

Then the Lord said to Moses, "See I have chosen Bezalel, son of Uri, the son of Hur, of the tribe of Judah, and I have filled him with the spirit of God, with skill, ability and knowledge in all kinds of crafts—to make artistic designs for work in gold, silver and bronze, to cut and set stones, to work in wood, and to engage in all kinds of craftsmanship." (Exodus 31:1-5)

Here's a trivia question for you: Who is the first person in the Bible described as being filled with the spirit of God? You might assume it's one of those hall-of-famers mentioned in the last chapter, but it's not. The first person said to be filled with God's spirit is a man named Bezalel, and the surprising thing is that Bezalel wasn't a preacher or a prophet; he was a carpenter, one who "engaged in all kinds of craftsmanship."

Bezalel was the chief architect of the tabernacle, called by God to oversee its construction and given special gifts of craftsmanship to make the tabernacle a place of beauty. Not only did Bezalel lead in the construction of the tabernacle, he also built the furniture that went inside it. He also designed the priestly garments to be worn there and extended his influence by teaching his art to others. Evidently, Bezalel was a multi-talented craftsman, for he was able to work with gold, silver, bronze, stone, and wood.

It was—and probably still is—a shocking thought that a workman, a carpenter, would receive the spirit of God to do his work. In the Greek and Roman cultures of that day, manual labor was despised. It was thought to be work for slaves, not free citizens. But in Hebrew thought, manual work was honored and esteemed. So, here in Exodus, we read about a manual laborer filled with God's spirit. The first person mentioned in Scripture as spirit-filled had sawdust in his hair and calluses on his hands.

Bezalel becomes a small hint of one to come. There would come a day when the God-Man, Jesus of Nazareth, would have sawdust in his hair and calluses on his hands. The very essence of God would walk the earth as a carpenter.

We need to know about Bezalel because he reminds us of something important: God fills people with the spirit to do more than *religious* things. People get filled with the spirit to build, paint, do accounting, raise children, write stories, and bake pies. Our calling as Christians is to become craftsmen and craftswomen for God, to let the work of our hands be a statement of our devotion. How we teach, sing, write, and tend our relationships are all statements of our love for God. We are to *care* about what we do.

Robert Capon wrote, "Culture can come only from caring enough about things to want them really to be themselves—to want the poem to scan perfectly, the song to be genuinely melodic, the basketball actually to drop through the middle of the hoop, the edge of the board to be utterly straight, the pastry to be really flaky. Few of us have many great things to care about, but we all have plenty of small ones."[1]

The poet W. H. Auden echoed that thought when he observed that while there might not be "Christian art,"as such, there most certainly is a Christian spirit that energizes and undergirds an artist's work. That's what God gave Bezalel—a spirit in which he designed his silver, cut his stones, and fashioned his wood.

Though we seldom think of ourselves this way, we are all artists for God. God fills us with the spirit so that we can be artists in the way we live, relate to people, and perform our duties. The old word for this is "stewardship," though we have sullied the word by talking about it only when we're describing the church budget. But "stewardship," in the best sense of the word, happens when we receive the spirit of God and become artists, committed to lives of excellence.

The writer Bruce Lockerbie wrote, "To serve Jesus Christ as an artist means offering to my Lord something that nobody else in the whole universe can give him—my own particular gift."[2] As we think about the work of our hands and being an artist for God, we realize that we can be good stewards only if we dare to make three commitments.

First, I will discover my gifts. As I said, those of us in the church have for too long thought of giftedness only in religious terms. We've thought that God gives gifts to people to preach, pray, counsel, administer a church, sing, play the piano, or comfort the grieving. God certainly gives those gifts, and they are indispensable for the church.

But Bezalel is a necessary corrective to the notion that God gives only religious gifts to people. Bezalel reminds us that God also gives the gifts of being a carpenter, mechanic, baker, engineer, homemaker, and poet. To be a faithful steward, we first have to discover our "thing." What can *I* do, love to do, feel called to do? Though we have a lot of fancy definitions for "faith," one we can all understand is this one: "Faith is finding out what we're here to do and then doing it with all of our heart."

Second, I will use my gifts to enhance the kingdom of God. We are gifted by God so we can help establish the kingdom of God on earth. We take our gifts and, like Bezalel, commit them to God and use them for God's kingdom.

The magnificent obsession of Jesus' life was the kingdom of God. He came into the world to establish this kingdom, which was a whole new way of approaching life. He recruited ordinary people to help him. He called fishermen, tax collectors, and housewives to catch this vision of a new kingdom and to help him build it. They would not be able to do big things, most of them, but they could do small things. They could take the work of their hands and use it to help fashion this kingdom of love and grace. Now you and I are in that lineage. We are construction workers for the kingdom of God.

Don't we need carpenters who will use their craftsmanship to build structures of style and beauty? Don't we need mechanics who will do honest work and keep our cars running efficiently? Don't we need teachers who will love children and see every child as "a thought of God"? Don't we need people who will bake peach cobblers and bring them to church suppers so that all of us can look forward to going? Don't we need a host of people who will see themselves as construction workers for the kingdom of God? God gave the spirit to Bezalel, and Bezalel, in turn, offered his gifts to God and to the people of God.

Third, I will make a commitment to develop my gifts and live a life of excellence. I'm sure that Bezalel's craftsmanship was honed through years of steady work. You don't get to be a craftsman by accident. Whatever our gift is, we get it in embryo form and have to nurture and develop it.

When I was in my twenties, I felt a strong nudge to try my hand at writing. I attended writer's conferences, read books on the craft of writing, and finally put pen to paper (that's what you did back in those pre-computer days!). My first attempts at writing a book were unsuccessful, and I stuffed my drawers with rejection slips. But I kept plugging, kept sending stuff out, kept trying to get better at putting words on paper.

Eventually, it paid off. Through the ensuing years, I've been able to write some books and articles and have felt a great joy through the whole process. As a writer, I'm still learning and developing. Occasionally, I'll read someone who fashions sentences of incredible style and impeccable grace, and I'm filled with envy. But my calling is not to be the best writer in the world; it's to be *the best writer I can be,* to hone my gift and become a writer of excellence.

That is what all of us are called to do. We're called to develop our gift, to polish our craft—be it fixing cars, teaching our Sunday school class, or taking care of our grandkids. Our goal is excellence, whatever our gift.

William Temple, former archbishop of Canterbury, once observed that God is not primarily concerned about religion, and Bezalel reminds us of that. The first person to be filled with the spirit of God was a craftsman, acquainted with blisters and sweat. He was filled with the spirit so he could offer God, and the people of God, the work of his hands.

There's an old and wonderful story from the life of Saint Francis. One afternoon, he said to his disciples, "Let's go out and preach." So, they went out and walked through the town and never said a word. When they got home, his disciples said, "I thought we were going out to preach." Saint Francis reportedly replied, "We did preach. *They saw us,* didn't they?"

They will see us, of course. They will see our stewardship, the way we live, the care we put into our activities, how we use our gifts.

The real question is: Will they sense the spirit of God when they see the work of our hands?

Notes

[1] Robert Capon, *Bed and Board* (New York: Simon & Schuster, 1965), 108-109.

[2] Bruce Lockerbie, *The Timeless Moment* (Westchester IL: Cornerstone Books, 1980), 119.

For Reflection and Discussion

1. Do you know your gifts? What are they?

2. How can you use your gifts to enhance the kingdom of God?

3. What steps should you take to develop your gifts?

4. Which people in your life help you sense the presence of God through the work of their hands?

5. Do you agree that God is not primarily concerned about religion? Why or why not?

STONES AND SNAPSHOTS

*These stones are to be a memorial to the people of Israel forever.
(Joshua 4:7)*

There's an old joke about a man who went to the doctor with a major memory problem.

"Doc, I have a problem," he said. "I can't remember a thing."

"How long have you had this problem?" the doctor asked.

"What problem?" the man replied.

The older I get, the less funny that joke becomes. But it can remind us that we all have a memory problem. We're all prone to forget God and the things that matter. The Israelites in the Old Testament wore phylacteries so they wouldn't forget God. They knew how easy it is to forget, so they tied Scriptures around their wrists and foreheads to jog their memory.

Our family doesn't wear phylacteries, but we have done what I suppose a lot of families do. We've taken pictures and stuffed them in albums so we won't forget who we are and where we've come from. Maybe, in some indirect way, so we won't forget God and how much God has blessed us.

We have more than thirty albums bulging with memories. The kids when they were babies. The kids on their first day of school. Christmases around the tree. Grandparents, cousins, friends, aunts and uncles. Football games, basketball games, birthday parties. It's all there, a treasure chest of memories and a visible record of who we are and what we've done. Sometimes, when our now-grown kids come home, we get out some of those picture albums and laugh, reminisce, and feel better.

What did people do before the invention of the camera? Well, one of the things the biblical people did was pile up stones—memorials, if you will—so they would remember significant events and places. We still do that today when we erect monuments, towers, and gravestones.

That's what the people of Israel did when they finally made it to the promised land after forty long years in the wilderness: "When the whole nation had finished crossing the Jordan, the Lord said to Joshua, 'Choose twelve men from among the people, one from each tribe, and tell them to take up twelve stones from the middle of the Jordan from right where the priests stood and to carry them over with you and put them down at the place where you stay tonight'" (Josh 4:1). They erected this memorial at a place called Gilgal, and it was to be "a memorial to the people of Israel forever" (Josh 4:7). That marker there at Gilgal served several purposes for the Israelites.

It reminded them to be grateful. Think of it: For forty long years, those people had been trudging through the wilderness on a journey marked by frustration and confusion. Do the math, and you'll see that they averaged a whopping five miles a year on this journey. It was a journey of about two hundred miles, and it took them forty years to make it. You could crawl backward faster than that! It's not hard to imagine the joy and gratitude they felt when they finally made it to Canaan.

Those stones piled up at Gilgal were symbols of their gratitude. Every time the Israelites saw them, they were to be grateful for the fact that they had made it to the promised land, made it past their wilderness troubles, made it past a hard time to embrace a new chapter in their history. Every one of those rocks shouted, "Thank you!"

I suppose that's what we're doing too when we get out the picture albums and start reminiscing. We're remembering so that we can be grateful. When we look at those pictures—the slumber party, the ski trip, the wedding, the game when he hit the home run—laugh and are filled with gratitude. It's a Gilgal kind of experience, and we need that from time to time. Whether stones or snapshots, we need something to remind us to be grateful.

But those stones piled up at Gilgal were more than gratitude markers. *They were also reminders that God would continue to be faithful to them.* Joshua said to the people,

> In the future when your descendants ask their fathers, 'What do these stones mean?' tell them, 'Israel crossed the Jordan on dry ground.' For the Lord your God dried up the Jordan before you until you had crossed over. The Lord your God did to the Jordan just what he had done to the Red Sea when he dried it up before us until we had crossed over. He did this so that all the people of the earth might know that the hand of the Lord is powerful and so that you might always fear the Lord your God." (Josh 4: 21-24)

Have you ever been through a time when you weren't sure you would make it? A time when you were carrying some burden you thought might be too heavy? A time when you were dealing with some crisis or worry that seemed overwhelming?

But then, some amazing things happened, or maybe just some ordinary things happened, but you made it. You found surprising strength. You felt an unusual sense of the presence of God in your trouble. To put it in biblical terms, you crossed your wilderness and made it to the promised land. Then you filed that experience in your memory so you could go back to it when you need it. Now when you face a similar agony, you can say, "The God who saw me through that bad time will see me through this one."

That is what those stones at Gilgal were for. Every time the people saw them, they would remember: "The God who got us through the wilderness is still with us. The God who opened the Jordan River so we could pass through unscathed is still on our side. If God could see us through *that*, God can no doubt see us through *this* too." Those stones at Gilgal would fill the people with gratitude as they remembered their past, but they would also fill them with hope as they considered their future.

There was a third thing, too, that those stones did for the people of Israel: *They reminded them that they were passing along a heritage to those coming behind them.* Did you catch that phrase in the passage I quoted earlier? Joshua said, "In the future, when your children ask you. . . ." Those stones were not just for that generation; they were for the generations to come as well. Those stones were for the children and grandchildren and people hundreds of years down the road.

Back in Deuteronomy, God had commanded them, "These commandments that I give you today are to be upon your hearts. Impress them on your children. Talk about them when you sit at home and when you walk along the road, when you lie down and when you get up. Tie them as symbols on your hands and bind them on your foreheads. Write them on the doorframes of your houses and on your gates" (Deut 6:6-9).

Those stones at Gilgal were an attempt to be true to that command. When children and grandchildren saw the stones, parents and grandparents would tell the story of that miserable journey across the wilderness, explaining how God had been faithful and the people had landed here, right on this spot. Those stones would provide a teaching moment, and the story could be passed from one generation to the next.

I firmly believe in the importance of stones and snapshots. Whatever it takes to remind us to be grateful, to count on the faithfulness of God, and to pass on a legacy to our children and grandchildren is worth the effort.

Let's take pictures, put stone markers in the back yard, visit old gravestones in the cemetery, tell stories and swap yarns, and establish and keep family traditions. Let's even wear phylacteries, if that's what it takes to remember God and the things that matter.

As I was reading this passage from Joshua 4 about the stones erected at Gilgal, I flashed back in my mind to a place I lived years ago. I worked at a children's home in Round Rock, Texas, and one day Sherry and I did a little exploring to learn some local history. We went down to Brushy Creek and saw a huge, round rock in the river. People on wagon trains saw that rock, the story goes, and called the place "Round Rock." The name stuck, and now Round Rock, Texas, is a large suburban community north of Austin. The rock is still there, and anyone wanting to explore local history can venture to Brushy Creek and see it.

The writer of Joshua, in telling of the rocks at Gilgal, said, "they are there to this day" (Josh 4:9). I hope they are. But even if those rocks have been demolished or eroded away, we still have the writer's words that have weathered the centuries to remind us what happened at Gilgal—and also to remind us that some things are significant enough to deserve a stone.

For Reflection and Discussion

1. Which times in your life deserved a stone? Did you erect a marker of some kind?

2. What wilderness experiences have you had to endure? How did God lead you to the promised land?

3. What are some of the most common reasons we forget God?

4. Which stones or snapshots do you visit regularly? Why do you go there?

5. What are some specific ways we can pass our Christian heritage to coming generations?

GETTING ON GOD'S GOOD SIDE

And Micah said, "Now I know that the Lord will be good to me, since this Levite has become my priest." (Judges 17:13)

In spite of those rocks at Gilgal, the people of Israel *did* forget God and the things that matter. The book of Judges records a sad time in the life of the nation of Israel, a time when the people didn't obey and worship God and even the judges who were ruling were corrupt and godless.

After Joshua died, no leader came forth to lead Israel, and to say the nation floundered would be putting it mildly. The first sixteen chapters in the book of Judges tell us about the succession of leaders who tried in vain to lead, and you get the idea that Israel teetered on the brink of anarchy and ruin. One verse in the book says it all: "In those days Israel had no king; everyone did as he saw fit" (Judg 17:6).

Beginning in chapter seventeen, the compiler starts to focus on ordinary people, to show, I suppose, that not only were the *leaders* corrupt, but the rank-and-file folks weren't any better. Chapters 17 and 18 focus on a man named Micah who gives us a prime example of how *not* to relate to God. In fact, that is true of the entire book. Judges is a lesson in how *not* to live.

The Micah story, in my shortened version, goes like this: Once upon a time, a man named Micah lived in the hill country of

Ephraim. He was not a model of virtue, by any means, and even stole eleven hundred shekels of silver from his own mother. When he confessed his crime to his mother and returned the money, she forgave him, then took some of the returned money and had a silver idol built for him. Micah put the idol in his house and felt most religious about it.

He felt so religious, in fact, that he decided to hire his own priest. A young Levite from Bethlehem in Judea came calling one day, and Micah said, "Live with me and be my father and priest, and I'll give you ten shekels of silver a year, your clothes and your food" (Judg 17:10). That was too good a deal to pass up, and the priest took the deal before Micah could rescind it. Micah was thrilled and said, "Now I know that the Lord will be good to me, since this Levite has become my priest" (Judg 17:13).

But even with an idol in his house and his own priest, Micah's future didn't unfold as planned. One day a roving band of Danite warriors happened upon Micah's house, saw his silver idol, and made a mental note that this might be a good place to pillage someday. They went back home, gave a full report to their friends, and before you could say "ransack," six hundred men from the clan of the Danites were paying a call on Micah and his new priest. They took the silver idol and other valuables from the house and hit the road. The new priest knew a winning team when he saw one and decided he would become *their* priest, so he left with them.

When Micah, who was not at home when the idol was taken, heard about all of this, he gathered up some men and gave chase. Once he caught that band of Danites, he knew he was in way over his head. What could he and his little band of men do against six hundred Danite soldiers? The text says, "Micah, seeing that they were too strong for him, turned around and went back home" (Judg 18:26). He might have been a little slow, but he wasn't stupid.

When the curtain closes on the story at the end of Judges 18, the warriors are still warring and the idol is being used in the house of God in Shiloh. Micah, we presume, is home licking his wounds, grateful to be alive.

That's a strange story, isn't it? It's a story we don't ever hear about, probably because we don't know what to do with it. What possible "lessons for life" can we learn from these odd characters in the book of Judges?

I think one of the prime lessons we can learn is how *not* to relate to God. The story can bring into focus our own Micah-like qualities, our own attempts to win God's approval by being religious. Micah thought if he could get an idol and his own priest, he'd be set for life. He thought he could get on God's good side through a series of religious deeds. But it didn't work for him, and it won't work for us either.

All of the "religious" things we do—prayer, worship, Bible study, giving, and all the rest—can't buy God's approval. We love God because God *first* loved us. Before we ever uttered a prayer, attended a worship service, opened a Bible, or put a check in an offering envelope, God loved us. Those disciplines enable us to express our gratitude for God's love, and they enable us to sense the presence of that love in our lives. But they have no purchasing power whatsoever. God's love is not for sale.

A good example is a person who decides to step out into the sunshine and revel in the beauty of the day. Going outside to hike, fish, or play golf doesn't make the day any prettier than it already is. The sun is shining whether the person goes outside to enjoy it or not. But that person can't fully appreciate it until he or she gets out in it, feels the warmth, breathes the air, smells the flowers, and maybe rolls around in the grass.

That's what our religious deeds and our spiritual disciplines do for us. They enable us to roll around in the wonder of God's love and to appreciate the fact that we have it. They even enable us to celebrate the fact that we couldn't have bought God's love even if we had had an expensive silver idol and a priest of our own.

This strange story about Micah in the book of Judges turns out to be relevant after all. In a religious, even superstitious culture like twenty-first-century America, Micah beckons us to remember two simple truths.

First, there really is nothing we can do to earn the love of God. It's free and unconditional. Revel in it. Jump up and down about it. Look at the cross and celebrate it. Shed tears at the wonder of it. But don't try to earn it.

Second, there is much we can do to express gratitude for that love. All of those fine spiritual disciplines we practice give us tangible ways to thank God for loving us first. When we worship, pray, study, and give, we're saying "thank you" in tangible ways. Life, lived with God, is one thank you after another.

To put it simply: We can't do one thing to earn the sunshine, but it sure would be foolish not to enjoy it.

For Reflection and Discusson

1. What idols do you have that make you feel religious and secure?

2. Do you agree that our religious activities can't earn God's approval? Why or why not?

3. Do you think twenty-first-century America is a religiously superstitious culture?

4. What are you doing to express your gratitude to God?

5. Are you enjoying the sunshine of God's unmerited love? What can you do to frolic in it even more?

NEWS TOO GOOD
TO FORGET

The king asked, "Is the young man Absalom safe?" Ahimaaz answered, "I saw great confusion just as Joab was about to send the king's servant and me, your servant, but I don't know what it was." The king said, "Stand aside and wait here." So he stepped aside and stood there. (2 Samuel 18:29-30)

Since we're out there in the sunshine, celebrating the incredible, unmerited love of God, let me introduce you to another "hidden treasure" character in the Old Testament. His name is Ahimaaz, and his story would be hilarious if it didn't hit so close to home. But there's something in his story that I hope will help us celebrate the amazing grace at the core of the Christian message.

Ahimaaz's story is told in 2 Samuel 18. He desperately wanted to be the king's courier, to carry a message to King David. Absalom, David's son, had died, and someone needed to carry that important news back to the king. Ahimaaz pleaded to be the one, but General Joab didn't think that was a good idea: "You are not the one to take the news today. You may take the news another time, but you must not do so today, because the king's son is dead" (2 Sam 18:20). Joab then dispatched a Cushite courier to take the news to the king.

But Ahimaaz was not to be denied: "Come what may, please let me run behind the Cushite" (2 Sam 18:22). Joab, no doubt sensing he was about to be pestered unmercifully, relented. "Run," he sighed, and Ahimaaz took off like an Olympic sprinter. He was so filled with enthusiasm that he outran the Cushite courier and beat him to King David.

There he was, standing before the king, his dream about to become a reality. He had finally become the king's courier. But what happened next is hard to fathom. Would you believe that Ahimaaz forgot the message? Or maybe he never really knew the message. Or maybe he got tongue-tied in the presence of the king he so admired. But, for whatever reason, he stuttered and stammered and couldn't deliver the news. He had to stand aside and wait until the Cushite arrived to tell David that Absalom had died.

That is the strange saga of a messenger who, when entrusted with an important piece of news, forgot what he was supposed to say. The saga would be humorous indeed if it wasn't so much like our situation in contemporary Christianity. We too have been entrusted with an important message, but all too often we forget what it is. We have become the descendants of Ahimaaz.

What do you think would be the best news human beings could hear? Think of it in terms of a headline, perhaps. What would be the most glorious headline you could imagine?

When I put my mind to it, I can think of some wonderful headlines:

Astros Sweep Yanks, Win World Series
Judson Edwards Book Soars to #1 on Bestseller List
World Hunger Problem Solved
Cure for Cancer Discovered
Doctors Reverse Opinion, Say Sugar and Fat Good for People

Try as we might, though, we can never top the news already announced in the pages of the New Testament: *God Reconciles the World through Christ.* That is the single most wonderful piece of news ever sounded on planet earth. God has set things right. We have been reconciled and restored through the person of Jesus Christ. All of the walls that separated people from God have been demolished.

That is not only the best news ever sounded, it is also the essence of the New Testament message. It ought to set our hearts to racing and our feet to tapping every time we hear it. But, somehow, we have forgotten the message. We must recover it, for it is a message too good to forget.

How do we lose it? How do we forget the one piece of news that can give people hope and set them free? I think we lose it in a number of ways, all subtle and all insidious.

We lose the good news any time we substitute theology for the gospel. I have spent a good portion of my life studying theology and believe it to be important. But I know that our attempts to understand and describe God are not the same as glad acceptance of God's grace. One is like analyzing the chemical elements in water; the other is like splashing in cool water on a hot day. *Studying* God and *experiencing* God are not synonymous.

We lose the good news any time we substitute morality for the gospel. Certainly, we ought to be moral people, but there isn't much good news in a moral code. The Christian message is not "be better people, try harder, and maybe you can win God's favor." The Christian message is "God has taken all of our sins and forgiven them in Christ, so live your life with freedom and joy." It's enough to make you weep in gratitude.

We lose the good news any time we substitute activism for the gospel. In an attempt to codify and organize everything (even God!), we can easily turn Christianity into a checklist of impressive things to do. We think if we can just do all of these religious activities (like Micah?), we will be pleasing to God. We make a mental list of all the things we need to do to win God's approval—go to church, tithe, witness, be a good parent, visit our lonely neighbor, and so forth. But where is the good news in an endless to-do list? When the Galatian Christians started compiling their list, the apostle Paul reminded them that they had "fallen away from grace" (Gal 5:4).

Finally, we lose the good news any time we substitute institutionalism for the gospel. All too easily the Christian life can become a burdensome series of church events and programs. We inadvertently turn the good news into a promotional campaign for the institutional church and become focused on raising money, building buildings, subscribing budgets, and formulating policies. The good news of free grace becomes the bad news of corporate bureaucracy.

Those substitutions for the gospel *are* subtle because they are all fine things. Theology *is* important. Morality *is* necessary. Spiritual activities *do* improve us and our world. The church *is* an institution, with all of the trappings of institutionalism. What we must remember, though, is that those fine things are not the gospel of Jesus Christ and not the heart of what we Christians are about.

Perhaps we can get things back in focus if we think of Christianity as a circus. On the fringes of the circus are the sideshows—the world's smallest man, the world's strongest woman, and so on. But these are *not* the main attractions of the circus. We pass by them on our way to the center ring where the good stuff happens.

Once we get to the center ring, we see what we really came to see—the trapeze artists flying through the air, the giant elephant with the elegant lady riding on top, and the lion tamer risking life and limb in the cage. Center ring is where the real action is.

Theology, morality, activism, and institutionalism are the sideshows of faith. We pass by them on the way to the center ring where we discover an empty cross and an empty tomb. There in the center ring we realize that our gospel is not about what we humans have done at all. It is about what *God* has done: God was in Christ, reconciling the world to himself. Once we get to the center ring, we realize that God has done something that surpasses any headline we could create. God has set us free and given us a reason to live with hope and gratitude.

This center ring news is so astounding that we dare not forget or garble it. This one piece of news is our reason for celebration and the one thing that separates Christianity from all other religions. Ours is a message of grace—not what we have to do for God but what God has already done for us—and, properly understood, it does set our toes to tapping.

One more illustration and then I'll leave poor tongue-tied Ahimaaz alone. Think of the difference between a transaction and a celebration. A transaction is when we go to the grocery store, toss items into our grocery cart, write a check, and take our stuff home. We've done our part, the grocery store has done its part, and a transaction has been completed.

A celebration, on the other hand, is when the grocer shows up unexpectedly at our doorstep with the unbelievable announcement that we've just won a year's worth of free groceries. We didn't do anything to deserve the prize; we were simply selected as the grand prize winner. We call our neighbors to tell them the news, and we throw a party to celebrate our incredible windfall.

At its heart, the Christian gospel is not a transaction but a celebration. God showed up at the doorstep of our lives in Christ and announced that we are eternal winners. Our part is to receive the gift and then spend the rest of our lives making merry. But, as I said, sometimes we forget, and when we do, our experience with God becomes anything *but* joy and merriment.

I think we are fighting a war in the church today between astonishment and boredom. We tend to draw many lines in church life—lines between liberals and conservatives, believers and unbelievers, Protestants and Catholics, and so on—but the line that matters most is the line between the astonished and the bored.

Sadly, we can be orthodox, moral, intellectual, and heavily involved in church and still be bored silly. Without astonishment, wonder, and surprise at what God has done for us in Christ, we become descendants of Ahimaaz. We arrive on the scene huffing and puffing, but we have forgotten the message. We are useless as couriers.

Let poor, stammering Ahimaaz be a constant reminder to us that important messages can be forgotten. And let us remember that the news we carry is much too good to forget.

For Reflection and Discussion

1. Do you agree that the church has forgotten its message of grace? Why or why not?

2. List some wonderful headlines you would like to see. Can any of them top the message of the New Testament?

3. The chapter mentions four ways we lose the good news. Which of the four is the most prevalent in your life? In the church?

4. Think of the difference between a transaction and a celebration. Which best describes your approach to faith?

5. What specific actions could you take to banish boredom and restore astonishment in your life?

WHICH PART
WILL YOU PLAY?

*Some time later there was an incident involving a vineyard belonging to
Naboth the Jezreelite. The vineyard was in Jezreel, close to the palace of
Ahab king of Samaria. (1 Kings 21:1)*

The story of Naboth's vineyard in 1 Kings reads like a drama. One
Bible scholar I read said the story is indeed a drama and that the
drama has six scenes structured in "chiastic parallelism." I was fascinated to discover that this story has "chiastic parallelism" and would
probably be even more fascinated if I knew what "chiastic parallelism"
was! Maybe it's one of those phrases scholars toss around to sound like
scholars.

But I do think the story reads like a play, and I agree with that
scholar that it seems to have six scenes:

Scene 1—Ahab, the King of Israel, lusts after the vineyard of
Naboth, the King of Samaria, and offers to buy it from him. Naboth
refuses the offer, though, because the vineyard is part of his family
inheritance.

Scene 2—Ahab trudges home, sullen and angry, because his offer
has been refused. He lies down on his bed and refuses to eat. When his
wife, Jezebel, asks him what is wrong, he tells her what has happened.
She scoffs that a king would be such a sullen wimp and vows to take
care of the matter herself.

Scene 3—Jezebel hatches a plot. She writes letters in Ahab's name to the elders and nobles in Naboth's city. The letters direct the city leaders to find two scoundrels who will accuse Naboth of cursing both God and the king and say he should be stoned to death.

Scene 4—The elders and nobles do exactly as the letter tells them to do. Naboth is falsely accused by two scoundrels, tried by the city leaders and found guilty, and then taken outside the city and stoned to death.

Scene 5—Jezebel hears what has happened and tells Ahab to get up and get the vineyard he's been coveting. He does precisely that and goes down to take possession of Naboth's vineyard.

Scene 6—The word of the Lord comes to Elijah and tells him to go confront Ahab and Jezebel about their sin. Elijah goes and speaks a word of doom to both of them, declaring that certain disaster awaits them and their descendants.

At the end of the drama, poor Naboth is in the grave, the city leaders, we presume, have gone back to other sinister dealings, Ahab and Jezebel are living under Elijah's curse, and Elijah is off to confront others in the name of God.

When we think of that biblical drama in 1 Kings, we can think of the roles in the drama and see how clearly defined they are in the text. We can even ask ourselves, if we dare, which role best fits us. Think of the story of Naboth's vineyard, and then ask the question, "Which part am I playing?"

There is the role of Naboth, *Innocent Victim*. As far as we can tell in the text, Naboth did absolutely nothing to deserve his fate. He was simply a victim of unscrupulous people. His death was tragic and completely unjustified.

The role of innocent victim is one we all play at some point in life. We didn't deserve the accident, the disease, or the misfortune, but it happened, and we were victimized. One reason the book of Job has always been popular is that so many people relate to Job's dilemma. He was an innocent victim blindsided by catastrophe, and so, at some point, are we all.

The role of innocent victim is not one we usually want, but, in an odd paradox, it is a role that is hard to give up once we have it. It's easy to settle into a lifestyle of victimization. Others shower us with sympathy. We don't have to assume much responsibility because, after all, we've been wounded. We can even justify some righteous indignation because life has been so unfair.

In short, the role of innocent victim is a role we'll all probably play during our lives, but it's not wise to get addicted to it.

Then there's the Ahab role, *Sullen Sulker.* Ahab wanted Naboth's vineyard, and when he didn't get it, he went to bed, refused to eat, and had a giant pity party. Is there anything harder to take than someone throwing a personal pity party? Even Jezebel, no model of virtue herself, was repulsed by her husband's sulking. "Is this how you act as king over Israel?" (1 Kgs 21:7), she asked incredulously.

Jezebel took matters into her own hands, which, come to think of it, is probably why we sulk in the first place. We're hoping someone will come to our rescue, assume responsibility for us, and deliver us from hard choices and hard work.

The role of sullen sulker is not one anyone should play for long. It keeps us stuck in immaturity and guarantees that other people will avoid us at all costs. Mature people don't gravitate toward pity parties or the people who throw them.

Then there's the role of the city leaders, *Soldiers of the System.* Those men were pragmatists whose motto seemed to be "We go along to get along." When you read the story, you can almost hear them thinking, "If the powers-that-be trump up some charges against Naboth and tell us to act on them, what can we do? We're just soldiers of the system. We're not here to make waves. We'd like to keep our seat on the city council, and disobeying people of power is not the way to do it. Besides, we've done a lot of good things for this city and hope to do even more."

"Just hammer the nails in his hands," the system said when Jesus went to Golgotha. And the soldiers did it.

That soldiers of the system role is one we all play at times too, but, as the old saying goes, all evil needs to get a foothold is a bunch of good people doing nothing. Get enough soldiers of the system together, "going along to get along," and evil will thrive.

Finally, there's the Jezebel role, *Wickedness Personified.* What can we say about Jezebel? She was domineering, conniving, greedy, dishonest, and violent. Her philosophy seemed to be "I'll take what I want whenever I want it," and Naboth got steamrolled in the process. Jezebel is a prime example of what happens to anyone who is fixated only on "me and mine."

Let's hope we never assume that wickedness personified role, but, if we're honest, we can all probably remember a few times when we acted a lot like Jezebel. When the apostle Paul said we've all sinned and fallen short of the glory of God, we know exactly what he meant.

By the time we've examined all the roles in the drama, it hits us that none of them makes for a good life script. We wouldn't choose any of those roles as the ideal role for the rest of our lives. No sensible person wants to be the *Innocent Victim*, the *Sullen Sulker*, the *Soldier of the System*, or *Wickedness Personified* for life. We might slide in and out of those roles from time to time, but if we get stuck in any of them, we know we're doomed to a life of misery.

The story of Naboth's vineyard gives us no role to which to aspire. Even when we add Elijah to the mix, his role of *Prophet of Doom* doesn't hold much intrigue either. At the end of the drama, we're left wishing for more, yearning for a model who would inspire us, a role that would captivate us.

I think what we really need is someone like Jesus, *Forgiving Friend.* Years ago, this Naboth text popped up in the lectionary, and I felt obligated to preach on it. The New Testament text for that Sunday was Luke 7, the passage where Jesus forgives the woman who anointed his feet with perfume in the house of Simon the Pharisee. I struggled with how those two passages fit together. What does the murder of Naboth in 1 Kings 21 have to do with Jesus forgiving the woman in Luke 7? Why would the lectionary writers link those two texts?

I finally decided that, at least for me, Jesus in Luke 7 came along to give me the role model I couldn't find in 1 Kings 21. After that sordid tale of victims, sulkers, soldiers of the system, and wickedness personified, I needed Jesus, the forgiving friend. The Naboth tale, with its greed, violence, and victimization, sounded too much like what I hear on the ten o'clock news. Jesus forgiving that sinful woman stood in stark contrast to the evil in the Naboth story and to the evil I see all around me. Luke 7 reminded me that I do have a role model after all. I can be a forgiving friend, like Jesus.

One of the longest running fallacies in the history of humankind is the idea that condemnation and criticism help people change. If we can just throw enough stones at people, we seem to think, they'll see the error of their ways and repent. So husbands criticize their wives, and wives criticize their husbands. Parents berate their children. Preachers harangue people from the pulpit. Denominations pass resolutions condemning society. We believe if we can spew forth enough condemnation, people will reform.

But condemnation has proven to be a poor motivator. It hasn't worked in the past, and it won't work in the future. Criticism doesn't heal. Only forgiveness has the potential to heal, and it might not work either. People might spurn our forgiveness, take advantage of it, even nail it to a cross. But Jesus' kind of forgiveness is our best hope for changing the world.

I once read that the organizers of the national spelling bee had to set up a "comfort room" where contestants could go and cry and vent their frustrations on a punching bag. These, of course, were children who were the best spellers in their school and city. They had spelled hundreds of impossible words correctly, but then misspelled one word, and their dream collapsed. Their destiny became the "comfort room."

I think of all the "failures" in our world—people who have failed at marriage, job, school, and parenting. People who didn't make the big leagues or the PGA tour. People who failed as singers, dancers, writers, and poets. Just ordinary failures, like you and me.

What do these people need? They need more than a "comfort room" and a punching bag. They need someone who will love them in their failures the way Jesus loved that woman in the home of Simon the Pharisee.

Which part will we play to all of those ordinary failures we see every day of our lives? The Naboth drama reminds us of several popular options—*Innocent Victim, Sullen Sulker, Soldier of the System,* and *Wickedness Personified.* But none of those roles will help that distraught failure in the comfort room.

He or she needs a *Forgiving Friend.*

For Reflection and Discussion

1. Have you ever played the role of *Innocent Victim?* Are you still stuck in that role?

2. Have you ever played the role of *Sullen Sulker?* What got you out of your self-pity?

3. Have you ever been a *Soldier of the System?* How do we let institutions rob us of our courage to do what is right?

4. Have you ever been *Wickedness Personified?* Even if you've never been as evil as Jezebel, do you sometimes become too dominant and controlling?

5. Have you ever been a *Forgiving Friend?* Are there people in your life right now who need you to be one?

PLAYING THE GOD GAME

Then the Lord answered Job out of the storm. He said: "Who is this that darkens my counsel with words without knowledge? Brace yourself like a man; I will question you, and you shall answer me." (Job 38:1-3)

We know the story of Job, how he lost everything, how his possessions, his health, and his family were all stripped from him. As I mentioned in the last chapter, that story is a familiar one, and we embrace it because we, too, eventually become innocent victims like Job.

What is *not* so familiar, though, is the way God responded to Job's plight. We would expect God to shower Job with sympathy and caress him with tenderness. But that's not what happened. Instead, God challenged Job. "Brace yourself like a man," God said to him. "I will question you, and you shall answer me."

That's exactly what happened. God hurled a series of questions at Job: "Where were you when I laid the foundations of the earth? Have you ever given orders to the morning, or shown the dawn its place? Have the gates of death been shown to you? Can you set up God's dominion over the earth? Do you send the lightning bolts on their way?" Those questions and dozens of others fill chapters 38 through 41. We can boil all of those questions down to one primary idea: "Job, where did you ever get the idea that you are God?" Job, in his grief, was playing the "God Game," and God called him on it.

It would be nice to dismiss those questions as ancient queries directed to one man and forget them. We would like to wag our heads in spiritual superiority and say, "How could Job have been so foolish? How could he have ever set himself up as God?" But honesty demands that we take the text more seriously than that. Honesty demands that we confess our tendency to play the "God Game" too.

Scratch around a little bit, and you will probably find it in your own life. The "God Game" revolves around the issue of control, and we desperately want to be in control of our lives. To put it more bluntly, we desperately want to be God.

A woman once asked a friend how she was doing. The friend replied, "My life is crazy right now. I hate losing control." The woman replied, "You don't hate losing control. You hate losing the illusion you were ever in control." We do hate losing that illusion, so we play the "God Game." We clutch the illusion of control to us like my son used to clutch his favorite baby blanket.

How do we play the "God Game?" Let me count the ways:

We play the "God Game" when we worry. That great passage in the Sermon on the Mount (Matt 6:25-34) where Jesus tells us not to worry is built upon the premise that we let God be God. He tells us to consider the birds of the air and the lilies of the field. God takes care of them; will God not also take care of us?

It sounds so inviting, but it's hard to do. We wring our hands, fret, and fume because we think *we're* in control, *we're* responsible, *we're* calling the shots. The only antidote to this stressful existence is to let God be God. As Jesus put it, "to seek first the kingdom of God" (Matt 6:33). The antidote to anxiety is the one God challenged Job to embrace: Get off the throne of the universe, and let God be God. Get things in the proper order, and your worry will melt like snow in the sunshine.

We play the "God Game" when we try to change people. When we look around us, we notice that some very ordinary people surround us. It doesn't take a genius to see that our husband or wife has some major flaws. Our kids don't like to clean their rooms. Our best friend has a tendency to embellish the truth. Our coworkers are lazy. It's so obvious what these people need to do to improve themselves that we take on their reformation as our personal project. We try to make them better, to get them to become what we think they should become. We envision ugly caterpillars morphing into gorgeous butterflies because of our influence.

But if we do that with enough people, we will eventually get out of the reformation business. We will learn that only God can change people, and we're not God. We will finally acknowledge the truth: all we can do is change *ourselves,* love the people around us, and let God transform their lives.

We play the "God Game" when we hoard things. Someone once defined a materialist as "anyone who has more things than I do." Materialism happens when we get addicted to owning. We acquire more and more stuff that we need less and less. The bottom line is this: we grow materialistic because we want to be God, to own everything, to reign supreme over our own kingdom.

Once again, the antidote to materialism is the willingness to let God be God. We practice the discipline of giving our money to remind ourselves that nothing is ultimately ours. Every time we give sacrificially to help someone else or put a check in the church offering envelope, we're acknowledging the sovereignty of God.

We play the "God Game" when we demand certainty. Like Job, we want our questions answered. We crave certainty and yearn for a black-and-white world without doubt, mystery, and ambiguity. It's hard to admit we don't know, hard to confess we are finite creatures in an infinite universe.

So we play the certainty game, offer easy answers to hard questions, spew trite spiritual formulas that promise to connect people to God, and spin proof texts for every dilemma life has to offer. We are God, we would like people to believe, and we have the answers.

We play the "God Game" when we fake perfection. I once heard of a church called "The Church of the Holy Innocents," and immediately

thought that's where I wanted to belong. I want to be holy and innocent, or, at least, I want you to think I am. I want to give the
impression I'm sinless and perfect, even though the Bible only offers
me the option of being sinful and forgiven. Our attempts to be spot-
less and righteous seem noble until we realize how easily they translate
into never needing forgiveness.

Our attempts to feign perfection are but another symptom of the
"God Game," and the sooner we confess our sins and admit our
humanity, the better off we'll be. Paradoxically, the better witness for
Christ we'll become.

By now, you've probably begun to see the common thread that runs
through all of these symptoms of the "God Game." In all of them,
everything revolves around *me*. Paul Tillich, the theologian, once
defined God as whatever is our Ultimate Concern, and all of these
symptoms exist when my Ultimate Concern is *me*.

> I worry because things aren't perfect for *me*.
> I try to change people because they don't meet *my* expectations.
> I hoard things so *my* life will be comfortable.
> I crave certainty so *I* can look authoritative.
> I want to look perfect so other people will admire *me*.

The "God Game" is all about *me*. This must have been what God
saw in Job. Sure, Job had legitimate sorrow and some honest questions, but he had crossed a line and had started drowning in self.
"Brace yourself," God said to him, "because I'm getting ready to show
you your real problem." The real problem wasn't his misfortune but his
inclination to play the "God Game."

It would be nice to be able to read this old story of Job and his
penchant for playing God and to sing, "It's Job, it's Job, it's Job, O
Lord, standin' in the need of prayer." But we can't sing it that way, not
if we have an ounce of self-awareness in us. We have to sing it the way
it was written: "It's *me*, it's *me*, it's *me*, O Lord, standin' in the need of
prayer."

Seemingly, Job got the message. After God had bombarded him with all of those questions in chapters 38 through 41, Job "got it." In chapter 42, Job says, "Surely I spoke of things I did not understand, things too wonderful for me to know." Then he said, "Therefore, I despise myself and repent in dust and ashes." Evidently, Job was willing to quit the "God Game."

Are we?

For Reflection and Discussion

1. Had you ever thought about God's challenge to Job? Is it surprising to you that God didn't give him comfort but challenge?

2. The chapter mentions five ways we play the "God Game." Which of the five is most tempting to you? Why?

3. Are there other ways we play the "God Game?" Think about other ways we try to play God.

4. What specific actions can we take to keep self from becoming our ultimate concern?

5. Have you ever had a personal sorrow and felt God didn't give you the comfort you needed? How did you handle that disappointment?

BRAGGING
RIGHTS

Walk about Zion, go around her, count her towers, consider well her ramparts, view her citadels, that you may tell of them to the next generation. For this is our God for ever and ever; he will be our guide even to the end. (Psalm 48:12-14)

I went to Home Depot recently and bought a drill. I was in the midst of a handyman project—attaching a new coffeemaker to the underside of a kitchen cabinet—and having a tough time. I bought the drill, put the coffeemaker in, and had no problems at all. I'm not sure I would have ever completed the project without that new drill. The amazing thing is that the coffeemaker is still there, several weeks after I installed it. That's a new record for me. I've decided I'm not as un-handy as I'm reputed to be; I've just never had the necessary tools a handyman requires.

In his book *Answering God,* Eugene Peterson says the psalms are the toolbox of the Christian faith:

> The Psalms are the best tools for working the faith—one hundred and fifty carefully crafted prayers that deal with the great variety of operations that God carries on in us. The Psalms attend to all the parts of our lives that are rebelling and trusting, hurting and praising. People of faith take possession of the Psalms with the same attitude and for the same reason that gardeners gather up rake and

hoe on their way to the vegetable patch and students carry pencil and paper as they enter a lecture hall. It is a simple matter of practicality—acquiring the tools for carrying out the human work at hand.[1]

I want to reach into that toolbox and pull out a psalm that is unfamiliar to many of us. Psalm 48 was written by the sons of Korah, who were musicians in the temple in Jerusalem. They wrote this hymn probably to be sung at one of the Jewish festivals. It's a hymn that celebrates the wonder of God, the city of Jerusalem, and the temple, and I'm hoping we can use it as a tool to help us see the wonder all around us too.

The psalm begins with this: "Great is the Lord, and most worthy of praise, in the city of our God, his holy mountain" (v. 1). This, obviously, is going to be a song for the mountaintop. In the toolbox that is the book of Psalms, we find a variety of tools. Some of them express anger, some doubt, some depression. But Psalm 48 is all about joy. The sons of Korah were asserting their bragging rights as children of God, citizens of Jerusalem, and worshipers in the temple. When I read Psalm 48, another hymn kept running though my mind: "Count your blessings, name them one by one. Count your many blessings, see what God has done."

The sons of Korah had the capacity to see it all through eyes of wonder. Others could ponder God and Jerusalem and the temple and see nothing wonderful at all. But these temple musicians who penned Psalm 48 were filled with amazement at what they saw all around them.

We know what that's like, don't we? When your child—your own flesh and blood, that child with her mother's eyes and her father's smile—takes her first step, that is a "wonder-full" thing. You tell the people at church or work about it, and they don't seem much impressed. They smile and nod and accommodate your enthusiasm, but they don't get it. To them it's just a first step. Don't all babies take a first step? But to you it's a miracle. To you it's headline material because you see it through the eyes of wonder and love.

Some of those ancient Israelites might have said, "It's just God. It's just Jerusalem. It's just a place of worship. What's the big deal?" But not the sons of Korah: "Walk about Zion, go around her, count her towers, consider well her ramparts, view her citadels, that you may tell them to the next generation. For this God is our God for ever and ever; he will be our guide to the end" (Ps 48:12-14).

Have you ever had the experience of being around someone who took delight in something you took for granted? African violets, perhaps. Or hummingbirds. Or old radios. Or stars. Because that person took delight in African violets, you started to see the beauty and wonder in them too. Or you noticed how breathtaking hummingbirds are. Or how fun old radios are. Or how fantastic it is to look through a telescope and see the stars. Wonder is always contagious, and when we're in the presence of it, we catch it too.

What Psalm 48 hopes to do is help us catch wonder. It's not trying to teach us anything or instruct us in theology. The sons of Korah wanted the readers of the psalm to become as fascinated with God and life as they were.

For that reason, it, and the other psalms in the toolbox that attempt to do the same thing, are required reading for all serious Christians. They're required reading because we "serious Christians" sometimes become *too* serious, and everything gets heavy, dull, and religious. I think the biggest temptation longtime Christians have is the one Psalm 48 is trying to prevent—the temptation to become overly familiar with all things ecclesiastical, to slide into apathy.

When I was in the fourth grade, I got my first pair of glasses, and I still remember the shock I had when I first put those glasses on. I looked out the window and was astonished at what I saw. I could read signs, see leaves on trees, and make out people's faces way down the street. With those new glasses on, I could actually *see*. Gradually, imperceptibly, my vision had grown fuzzy, and I hadn't known it.

Something like that can happen to us spiritually. Gradually, imperceptibly, we grow bored and apathetic, and we don't even notice it. We slip into spiritual lethargy—one hymn, one sermon, one Bible story at a time. It all becomes so familiar that we lose the wonder of it all. When we lose the wonder, we're destined for even more apathy. A vicious cycle is set into motion—familiarity breeds apathy, which breeds more familiarity, which breeds more apathy, ad nauseam. Let that cycle run too long, and we can become spiritually dead and not even know it.

I was flipping through my family tree recently and came across an interesting name. One of my ancestors was named "Laodicea Bailey." A note under her name said she went by the nickname "Dicey." I wouldn't want to be called Laodicea either! Do you remember that name from the book of Revelation? The church at Laodicea was the one that was neither hot nor cold, the one Jesus wanted to spew out of his mouth.

When we lose the wonder of it all, our name becomes "Laodicea." We become neither hot nor cold, just bored to tears. Our effectiveness as witnesses of the good news becomes "dicey."

Occasionally, people call our church to inquire as to the kind of church we are. I usually use the current terminology and describe us as a "moderate" Baptist church. But I really don't like that term. "Moderate" sounds like "Laodicean," like we're neither hot nor cold, just moderate. I want all of the positives being "moderate" implies: open-mindedness, accepting of differences, not fundamentalist, willing to let women serve however God calls them, thoughtful in interpreting the Bible, and so on. But I don't want our church to be tepid. If moderate means apathetic, we ought to find another adjective to describe ourselves.

I want our church's faith, and my own faith, to be warm, passionate, evangelistic, and wonder-full. I want to stay fresh, alive, and grateful. I want to live in Psalm 48 and have the same spirit as the sons of Korah. I want to see my church, my city, my God the way they saw theirs.

And I want my wonder to be grounded in the same assurance that gave energy to theirs: "For this God is our God for ever and ever; he will be our guide to the end" (Ps 48:14).

Note

[1] Eugene Peterson, *Answering God* (San Francisco: Harper & Row, 1989), 2-3.

For Reflection and Discussion

1. Have you ever known someone like the sons of Korah? How did that person maintain a sense of wonder?

2. Have you ever had a wonder-full experience that others didn't share? What was it, and how did you cope with it?

3. Do you agree that we Christians sometimes become too serious? What can we do to become less serious?

4. If someone asked you to describe your church, what terms would you use?

5. Do you feel a sense of wonder about your God, your church, your town or city? What would it take to renew a sense of wonder in your life?

FILLED WITH DELIGHT

I was filled with delight day after day, rejoicing always in his presence, rejoicing in his whole world and delighting in mankind. (Proverbs 8:30-31)

In his book *Orbiting the Giant Hairball,* Gordon McKenzie tells of the times his father would visit a cousin out in the country. His cousin had a trick he called "mesmerizing the chickens," and the trick went like this: The cousin would draw a chalk line on the front porch of the house and put a chicken on it. Then he would hold the chicken's beak on the chalk line, and, amazingly, the chicken would stay right there, never moving, as if stuck to that line. Even when the cousin removed his hands, the chicken would keep his beak on the line. McKenzie said that cousin would mesmerize up to seventy chickens at a time, so the front porch of the house would be filled with mesmerized chickens, all with their beaks glued to the chalk line.

That story reminded me of a saying I once heard: "Life is like a dogsled team. If you're not the lead dog, the scenery never changes." Sadly, that's true. All too often we become like those mesmerized chickens, nose to the chalk line, the scenery never changing. Unlike the sons of Korah, we live without wonder.

That's why this next passage is a good one to know. Proverbs 8:30-31 serves as the perfect companion passage to Psalm 48. The writer of Proverbs sang in perfect harmony with the sons of Korah. Life is to be lived with delight, he said. A wise person is "filled with delight day after day."

Throughout the book of Proverbs, the writer personifies wisdom. Wisdom walks, talks, and instructs. When we read parts of Proverbs, we get to listen to Wisdom itself and learn from the master. That's what happens in Proverbs 8. Through the entire chapter, Wisdom teaches us how to live.

Plato once said that wisdom has four parts: integrity, justice, fortitude, and temperance. The writer of Proverbs, in these two verses, says that wisdom has four parts, too, and he spells them out in rapid succession:

The wise person is filled with delight day after day. "I was filled with delight day after day," Wisdom exults. Albert Einstein reportedly said that there are only two ways to live your life. One is as though *nothing* is a miracle. The other is as though *everything* is a miracle. Wisdom says to opt for the second way.

Some days, it's easy to take delight. As I sit here at the computer typing these words, I'm looking out at the beauty of the Oregon countryside. It's early in the morning, sixty degrees outside, and I'm gazing at tree-covered hills, cows grazing in the pasture, a vegetable garden bursting with life, hummingbirds zipping around the feeder, and a neighbor's barn roof emblazoned with the word "Jesus." I've had my coffee, there's nothing to do today but write these words, and my blood pressure is probably at an all-time low. Who couldn't take delight on a day like today?

But there's coming a day when the sabbatical will end, and I will have to return to "the real world." That world has meetings, sermon preparation, hospital visits, weddings, funerals, and all of the other things a pastor does. In short, "the real worldloaded with stress. Will I be "filled with delight" when I get back home? Will I be able to treasure the routine, the work, the people there? I can only hope and pray that will happen. If I have any wisdom in me at all, it will.

Even in "the real world," far removed from cows, hummingbirds, and silence, Wisdom beckons me to be "filled with delight day after day."

The wise person always rejoices in God's presence. "Rejoice always in his presence," Wisdom tells us, and, in doing so, gives us the reason we can be filled with delight even when we're not on sabbatical. Back home, back in "the real world," God's presence can be felt. God is there—in those ordinary, routine days—so those days can be filled with delight too. The good news for people trapped in ordinary routines is that delight has less to do with scenery than with Spirit.

All of the classic spiritual disciplines exist to sharpen our awareness of the spirit of God around us. We worship, pray, study, meditate, fast, give, and serve not to win God's love but to make us aware of God's presence. The spiritual disciplines are for *our* benefit. Without them, we fail to see the delight in our routine.

Right now, we're surrounded by swirling sound waves. They're in this room as I type these words, and they're in the room where you're reading them. But we don't see them, hear them, or feel them and could assume they're not here at all. Plugging in a radio, however, would make the invisible obvious: the sound waves are here all right; we just haven't had the device we needed to hear them.

That's the way it is with God, I suspect. God is in this room, and God is in your room, but we are typically oblivious to God's presence. The spiritual disciplines are the "radio" that enables us to notice that God is with us. To alter Einstein's observation slightly, there are two ways to live your life. One is to see God *nowhere*. The other is to see God *everywhere*. Wisdom advises us to "rejoice always in his presence."

The wise person rejoices in the whole world. "Rejoice in his whole world," Wisdom says. Not just the sabbatical world where all is wonderful and well, but the *whole* world. Rejoice in the whole world because God's presence is in the whole world. In fact, God's presence is in *all* of the worlds that whirl around us.

Have you ever thought of life as offering each of us a myriad of worlds? Not just one world, but thousands of worlds. We're invited to notice those worlds and to take delight in as many of them as we would like.

Enter, if you want to be fascinated, the world of plants. Think of all the beauty there, all the truths to be learned, all the fun to be had. Some people have entered that world far more deeply than I have, and they have become those around whom I catch fascination. The plant world, like all the other worlds out there, is a world bursting with possibility.

Or think of the world of birds. Up here in Oregon, we're getting to see birds we never see in Texas. Yesterday, a grosbeak landed on the bird feeder out our back window. It had an orange breast and black wings lined with white stripes. It was beautiful, and we ran next door to ask our hosts what kind of bird it was. The hummingbirds buzzing outside my window are different from our Texas hummingbirds too. It's a whole new world up here when it comes to birds, one we hope to explore more fully in the coming days.

Then there's the world of stars. And the world of sports. And the worlds of dance, music, art, and food. There are more worlds around us than we can possibly imagine. Our job is not to name them all, or even live in them all, but to rejoice in them all. Wisdom "rejoices in his whole world."

The wise person delights in mankind. Wisdom saves the hardest task for last. It is not always easy to be filled with delight day after day, to rejoice always in the presence of God, or to rejoice in the whole world. But it is certainly not easy to delight in mankind. The fourth part of wisdom, though, is to do just that, to take delight in the people around us.

That is always easier said than done. I have jokingly told people that being a pastor would be a great job if it weren't for the people. I'm guessing that teachers, doctors, lawyers, and anyone else dealing with the public would echo that sentiment. People can be a pain! But there are also people without whom our lives would be impoverished, people who make our lives worth living.

Carlyle Marney, a longtime Baptist pastor, once likened our lives to a house. He said each of us is a house—some a sophisticated kind of house, some a fancy house, some a simple and functional house. He said our house has a number of rooms and a basement that contains the plumbing and the trash.

Marney also said that every house has a balcony, and on that balcony there are people sipping iced tea. These balcony people are the strong, positive influences in our lives—parents, grandparents, friends, sports heroes, a former coach, a fourth grade teacher. These people, Marney said, are our personal saints, and from time to time, we need to have an All Saints Day to give them their due. These balcony people have made us who we are, have seen us through our dark days, and deserve more credit than we usually give them.

These are the people who enable us to "delight in mankind." Without them, we might decide that people are more of a pain than a pleasure and opt for a life of seclusion. But because of our "balcony people," we can face the world, buoyed by the support of these who have loved us.

Put those four phrases together—filled with delight, rejoicing in God's presence, rejoicing in the whole world, and delighting in mankind—and you get the Proverbs concept of wisdom. It has nothing to do with IQ, educational achievement, social status, or bank account. This approach to wisdom is all about delighting and rejoicing. The person who is filled with delight day after day, rejoices always in God's presence, rejoices in the whole world, and delights in mankind is considered by the writer of Proverbs to be the epitome of wisdom.

But wisdom in any age is not easy to come by—especially if we've been mesmerized by a job, a school, a church, or a culture. There's a certain amount of security in standing on the chalk line, nose down, never looking around to see other options. There isn't much freedom or joy on that chalk line, but there *is* a lot of security.

A *Garfield* comic strip a few years ago showed Garfield leaping, Rambo-like, into a pet shop. He announced himself as "Freedom Fighter" and raced through the shop, flinging open the doors of the cages and shouting, "You're free! You're free!" Instead of jumping to their freedom, the cats and dogs and birds stayed in their cages, intimidated by the unknown possibilities that awaited them out there in the world of freedom.

Seeing this, Garfield surmised, "Hmmm, folks must not be heavily into freedom these days." So he walked back through the pet shop, slamming cage doors and proclaiming, "You're secure! You're secure!" The pets, reconfined, looked relieved.

Any person who decides to pursue the concept of wisdom outlined in Proverbs 8 might be looked upon as a bit eccentric. Imagine being filled with delight day after day. Imagine rejoicing in the presence of God. Imagine rejoicing in the whole world. Imagine delighting in mankind. That kind of person would look strange in a society of mesmerized chickens.

However, given a choice between security and freedom, wouldn't you rather be free? Given a choice between conformity and joy, wouldn't you rather have joy?

Honestly, where would you rather live—on the chalk line or in the mindset of Proverbs 8?

For Reflection and Discussion

1. Do you ever feel like a mesmerized chicken? What puts you on the chalk line?

2. In your "real world," how do you find delight day after day?

3. What do you do to hear God's sound waves? What enables you to rejoice in God's presence?

4. Have you discovered any "new worlds" recently? What "new world" is causing you to rejoice right now?

5. Think of the "balcony people" in your life. Is it time to have an "All Saints Day" and give them their due?

LOOKING FOR
THE ONE I LOVE

All night long on my bed I looked for the one my heart loves;
I looked for him but did not find him. (Song of Songs 3:1)

If you were to take a poll asking Christians to name the strangest book
in the Bible, I'm guessing the Song of Songs would get a lot of votes.
It is unlike any other biblical book, and the church hasn't always
known what to do with it. It is filled with eroticism and seems to be
nothing more than an embarrassing love note passed between two
young lovers.

But one way Christians have interpreted the Song of Songs is to
read it as an allegory. When read that way, it becomes more than a love
letter between a man and a woman; it becomes a person's attempt to
woo the Divine Lover. For centuries, some Christians have seen the
Song of Songs as one person's attempt to romance God.

Eugene Peterson, in his book *Five Smooth Stones for Pastoral Work,*
wrote,

> The love lyrics of the Song are a guard against every tendency to
> turn living faith into a lifeless "religion." They make sure that as we
> proclaim the truth *of* God, we do not exclude faith *in* God. The
> Song provides correctives to our tendencies to reduce faith to a tra-
> dition, or to make an academic dogma of it. It insists that however

impressive the acts of God and however exalted the truths of God, they are not too great or too high to be experienced by ordinary people in the minutiae of everyday life.[1]

In short, the Song of Songs, interpreted this way, rescues a relationship with God from "dryness." Meeting God, it says, is not like reading a book or solving a puzzle; it's like falling in love. In this view, the spiritual life is not primarily about theology or morality; it's about romance. It's about meeting God and falling madly in love.

In chapter 3 of the Song, the female character speaks of her relationship with the Divine Lover and, in the process, describes some characteristics of a life lived with God. The Song of Songs turns out to be a good guide for us as we try to learn about the spiritual life.

She first says something about *the difficulty of the spiritual life.* "All night long on my bed I looked for the one my heart loves; I looked for him but did not find him. I will get up now and go about the city through its streets and squares; I will search for the one my heart loves. So I looked for him but did not find him" (Song 3:1-2).

Who among us can't identify with those words? Haven't we too looked in vain for the Divine Lover? Haven't we too yearned for more intimacy with God? Haven't we too looked for God and been frustrated that God is so elusive?

When I was in seminary, I sat one day in the recliner in our tiny cracker-box house and invited the Divine Lover to come see me. I was tired of working off of hopes and hunches. I needed proof. If I was going to commit myself to a life of ministry, I needed God to come out in the open and tell me straight out I was on the right path. I promised God that my zeal would eclipse even that of the apostle Paul's if I could just have my own Damascus Road experience.

I sat in that recliner, waiting patiently for the Divine Lover to come. I was hoping for thunder, lightning, and a voice from heaven, but I would have settled for a still, small voice. Nothing happened. At least, nothing like I wanted. I sat there in silence for several hours, and my Suitor never showed up. Finally, I got up in frustration and resumed life. I decided to stay on the path of ministry, but I knew this

Lover wouldn't come at my command. I knew I would have to rely on hints and hunches more that I wanted to.

The spiritual life is difficult. God seldom shouts. If the Divine Lover says anything at all, it's in a whisper. But that doesn't sell well in a culture hooked on easy answers and quick fixes. Give us three points, all beginning with the same letter, and we're happy. Tell us of a formula for effective prayer or draw us a diagram of how the Holy Spirit works, and we're thrilled. When it comes to God, we want something tangible.

But God isn't tangible; God is mystery. That's one of the lessons of the Song of Songs. This Lover is elusive, and we need to know that before we enter the relationship.

Of course, we can deny it. We can pretend we have all the answers and that God chats with us on a regular basis. We can act as if the Lover shows up every time we beckon. In our heart of hearts, though, we know that's not true. We know this relationship is on the *Lover's* terms, not our own.

When we deny the difficulty of the spiritual life, we become dishonest, shallow people. Mark Twain once described the Platte River as a mile wide and an inch deep. There is a Platte River brand of Christianity that makes people wide but not deep, and without depth, that brand of Christianity one day withers and dies.

The Song calls us to be honest. We don't always get Who or what we want in this romance. We're not in control here; we're just caught in a maddening love affair.

The woman caught in this romance also alludes to *the companionship of the spiritual life.* "The watchmen found me as they made their rounds in the city. 'Have you seen the one my heart loves?'" (Song 3:3). She was wandering the streets, looking for her Lover, when these watchmen showed up to help. She felt secure enough in their presence to ask if they had seen her Lover. At least she didn't have to look all by herself.

Thankfully, the spiritual life is a life of companionship. We have watchmen out there who will join us in the search for the Lover. That's what church is for. That's why we join prayer groups and book clubs. That's why we drink coffee with friends. Those are our watchmen, united with us in a common search. With them, we share experiences, insights, ponderings, and love. With them, we get the assurance that others are searching for the Lover too and the hope that our common search will not be in vain.

Of course, sometimes the watchmen aren't particularly helpful. Sometimes they can even be harmful. Later in the Song, the woman tells of another search for the Lover: "The watchmen found me as they made their rounds in the city. They beat me, bruised me; they took away my cloak, those watchmen of the walls!" (Song 5:7). It's possible to fall in with bad watchmen who beat and bruise us spiritually and emotionally.

But good watchmen provide us the companionship we need to continue our search. Where would we be, for example, without the biblical writers who have written compellingly of their experiences with God? Where would we be without authors who have written with grace and truth and pointed us toward the Lover? Where would we be without friends, preachers, professors, Sunday school teachers, and others who have encouraged us and been honest with us as we tried to find God?

The writer of the Song would remind us that we are not alone out there in the night. We have watchmen around us who will give us companionship and even join us in the search.

Finally, the woman looking for her Lover expresses *the ecstasy of the spiritual life.* "Scarcely had I passed them when I found the one my heart loves. I held him and would not let him go till I had brought him to my mother's house" (Song 3:4). The good news in the Song of Songs is that the Lover is not totally inaccessible. He occasionally gets found and even gets to be held. There is an ecstasy in this relationship that makes the search for the Lover well worthwhile.

Couldn't that be our testimony too? Yes, the Lover is elusive, but there have been those moments—in a particular worship service, in the look in the eyes of an old woman, in the feel of the wind on our face, in the hope that blossomed after a tragedy, in a verse of Scripture that hit us right in the heart—that let us know this romance is well worth whatever we have to do to keep it alive.

When Jesus described the spiritual life, he spoke of it as a treasure hidden in a field and a pearl of great price (see Matt 13). But in those stories, the treasure gets found and brings great joy to its finder, and the pearl gets found too and is worth more than everything the man owned. The treasure and the pearl don't get found easily in Jesus' stories, but they *do* get found. Their unsurpassable value more than validates the search.

Robert Frost once said all good poetry begins with a lump in the throat. So does all good spirituality. At least that's what the Song of Songs seems to say. The woman narrator in chapter 3 has difficulty finding her lover, gets encouraged by watchmen as she scours the streets, and then finally sees him. That's all it takes to make her know the hunt is worth it—that lump in her throat when she sees him, that pounding in her heart, that desire to hold him close and never let him go.

Once you've caught even one glimpse of this Divine Lover, you know you've found the Love of Your Life.

Note

1 Eugene Peterson, *Five Smooth Stones for Pastoral Work* (Atlanta: John Knox Press, 1980), 33-34.

For Reflection and Discussion

1. Has there ever been a time when you searched in vain for God? How did you respond?

2. Are you skeptical of people who seem to be able to chat with God on a regular basis?

3. Who are some of the watchmen in your life who have helped you look for the Divine Lover? Are they always helpful?

4. Do you think most religion today is honest?

5. How and when did you first fall in love with God?

DO YOU SEE WHAT I SEE?

Arise, shine, for your light has come, and the glory of the Lord rises upon you. (Isaiah 60:1)

Do you ever secretly fear that some of the things you hear at church aren't true? Do you ever have the sneaking suspicion that some of the things we preach and sing are just wishful thinking? Do you ever privately harbor some skepticism and cynicism about songs, sermons, and even Bible verses?

I have a feeling that some of the people who first read Isaiah 60 felt that way. I think not everyone who first heard or read Isaiah 60 "bought into it."

Some of the people of Judah, no doubt, had become cynical and skeptical during their long exile in Babylon. They had been uprooted from their homeland, carried off into a foreign country, and separated from family and friends. Seventy long years had passed, and the ones who had not died during that seventy-year exile finally got to go home.

But they discovered that "home" wasn't what it used to be. Buildings had been torn down and the temple destroyed. The economy was in shambles, and it was impossible to find work. It was a depressing, discouraging, dead-end time.

When the prophet of God said to those people, "Arise, shine, for your light has come, and the glory of the Lord rises upon you," some of them probably rolled their eyes and wondered at his silly piety.

"What world is he living in?" they scoffed.

"Some light!" others sneered as they surveyed the wreckage around them.

"If this is the glory of the Lord, I'd hate to see his punishment!" they probably said.

But the prophet wanted them to see their world through different eyes, through eyes of faith and hope. "Do you see what I see?" he was asking them. "Will you *dare* to see what I see? Will you look for God in this depressing situation?" The prophet saw the same darkness they saw, but he saw it through eyes of faith: "See, darkness covers the earth and thick darkness is over the peoples, but the Lord rises upon you and his glory appears over you" (Isa 60:2).

Let me ask you a personal question: When you look around you, and inside you, what do you see? When you take an inventory of your past, assess your present, and calculate your future, what do you come up with?

Certainly, there is much we *don't*, or *can't*, see. Neurological experts tell us our brains are equipped with a reticular activating system that serves as a filter. If all of the sensory stimuli we see, hear, and touch actually entered our brain, we would "flip a breaker," so the brain has a mechanism to filter out much of that stimuli. Most of what we see, hear, and touch gets filtered out before it ever makes it to our brain. We never become conscious of it.

Recently, Sherry asked me if I had seen the glue anywhere. I gave it some serious thought and told her that no, I hadn't seen the glue in a long time. It turned out that the glue was in my top desk drawer, a drawer I open several times every day. Every day I looked at that glue and didn't see it. My reticular activating system determined that I didn't need to notice that glue, so it filtered it out before it ever came to my consciousness. Experiences like that make me wonder how many other things get filtered out before I notice them.

One of the finest things the Bible does for us is remind us that God is a factor in reality. It keeps telling us not to forget God. When we assemble all of the data about our lives and our future, the Bible reminds us not to let God get filtered out of the mix. It keeps telling us that those divine sound waves truly are swirling all around us.

That's how I interpret a passage like Isaiah 60. He wasn't just giving those sad people a pep talk. He wasn't just offering them sweet piety or wishful thinking. Isaiah 60 was the prophet's way of reminding those disconsolate people, "There is a part of reality you're not seeing. Filter God out of the mix, and things look pretty bleak. But put God in the mix, and surprising things start to happen."

There is an Old Testament incident that portrays this truth memorably. It's in 2 Kings 6, and it focuses on a servant of the prophet Elisha. One morning this servant woke up, looked out the window, and immediately felt his heart in his throat. While they were sleeping, the enemy had come and encircled the village of Dothan. He went running to his master, Elisha, with the panic-stricken cry, "O, my Lord, what shall we do?" (2 Kgs 6:15).

But Elisha looked out at the same enemy and said to the servant, "Don't worry, those who are with us are more than those who are with them" (2 Kgs 6:16). Then he prayed a prayer asking God to open the servant's eyes so he could see the horses and chariots of fire on their side. The Lord opened the servant's eyes, and he saw the horses and chariots of fire and knew all would be well.

I have liked that story for years because I think it's *our* story. Some mornings we wake up, look out the window, and are terrified. In the dark of night, the enemy has surrounded our house, and, standing at the window in the early morning hours, we tremble at what we see— a job we dread, a person we abhor, a sickness that threatens our future, a boredom that sabotages our joy, a confusion about who we are and where we're going, or something else that looks menacing. That enemy, whoever or whatever it is, threatens to overwhelm us.

But that story in 2 Kings 6 asks, "Have you filtered God out of the mix so that you can't see the horses and chariots of fire on your side? Have you, by chance, lost sight of all the resources available to you if only you will tap into them?"

I know there are times when the Christian message sounds like wishful thinking. I know saying "all things work together for good to those who love God" is like putting a bandage on a malignant tumor when you're really suffering. I know life doesn't always have quick fixes and easy answers. And I know people sometimes get in situations that seem hopeless.

But I also know this: our story declares that God has taken the worst possible situation and made something good of it. Can you think of a worse situation than the one Jesus was in? He was a young man in his early thirties. He went about doing good but was rejected by nearly everyone around him. He was framed by the religious and judicial systems of his day, falsely convicted of a crime, and sentenced to die the cruelest death anyone can imagine.

Take all of that and add it up. What do you get? Despair? Anger? Depression? Catastrophe? You would assume so. Except there are some horses and chariots of fire in the story, some hidden forces at work that transform the whole experience into something miraculously positive. And this—the injustice, the rejection, the cruelty, the death—amazingly adds up to salvation, victory, and grace.

That story, for Christians, is the paradigm that determines our view of reality. That story shapes and informs our faith and keeps reminding us that God can take the worst possible scenario and redeem it, resurrect it, transform it. Once that story gets into our bloodstream, we become people of hope. If God can transform even a crucifixion, what might he do with the wreckage in *my* life?

Long before Jesus was crucified and resurrected, the prophet in Isaiah 60 wanted his listeners to factor a transforming God into the equation of their disaster. Sure, it was a dark time. Sure, broken things littered the countryside and their hearts. But the prophet reminded them not to sell God short: "Lift up your eyes and look about you: All assemble and come to you; your sons come from afar, and your daughters are carried on the arm. Then you will look and be radiant, your heart will throb and swell with joy" (Isa 60:4-5).

With God, nothing is impossible. With God, cruel crosses become glorious resurrections. With God, disillusioned, heartbroken people become radiant, and their hearts start to throb and swell with joy.

For Reflection and Discussion

1. Do you ever secretly fear that some of the things you hear at church aren't true? If so, what do you do with your doubts?

2. When you are in the midst of depression, discouragement, and desolation, what helps you see the light and glory?

3. Have you ever seen the horses and chariots of fire on your side? What was the occasion for their appearance?

4. Can you think of a situation in your life when a seemingly hopeless situation worked out for good?

5. If the cross and resurrection are our paradigm for reality, what implications can we make for our lives?

THE WILDERNESS MOTEL

O, that I had in the desert a lodging place for travelers, so that I might leave my people and go away from them; for they are all adulterers, a crowd of unfaithful people. (Jeremiah 9:2)

Imagine that someone you love dearly is on a collision course with disaster. Maybe it's a son or daughter; maybe it's a friend. But this special person is self-destructing. You know how it's going to end. You know this person is going to get hurt, maybe even die, unless someone intervenes.

You also know that "someone" is you. You feel you need to do something, even though you know this person will have to make the necessary changes on his or her own. But you know you need to say or do something, because silence would be indifference, and you are not indifferent about this person. You would rather eat nails than get involved in this tawdry situation, but you know you have to. So you tiptoe into it with fear and trembling.

That, or something like that, is what Jeremiah felt when God called him to be a prophet. He is known as "the reluctant prophet" because he didn't really want to get involved in Judah's tawdry situation. Unlike Isaiah, who said an eager "Here am I, send me" when God called him, Jeremiah, in effect, said, "Surely not me, Lord. Get someone else." He tiptoed into his prophetic role with fear and trembling.

But Jeremiah did enter the fray, and it was a rocky road all the way. He probably suffered more than any other Old Testament prophet and continually complained about his fate. In chapter 9, he expresses a desire to "chuck it all" and run away. He yearned for a little motel in the desert, a place where he could operate far away from the pressures of being a prophet: "O, that I had in the desert a lodging place for travelers, so that I might leave my people and go away from them . . ." (Jer 9:2).

If I were to try to give a modern paraphrase of Jeremiah's desire, it would go like this: "Oh, that I could find a little motel out in the Hill Country of Texas. Kerrville, maybe. Or Mountain Home. Just a place where I could take it easy, drink coffee with farmers at the local café, maybe even play dominoes with the old guys in the park. I wouldn't need to make a lot of money at the motel, just enough to put food on the table. But I'd be able to relax. My blood pressure would go down. I might actually remember how to laugh. And I would never again have to be the resident spokesman for God."

Jeremiah wanted to go where Henry David Thoreau went: "on the promenade deck of the world, an outside passenger, where I have freedom in my thought and in my soul am free." That would have been glory for Jeremiah. Even a casual reading of the prophecy that bears his name reveals why he needed the wilderness motel. He had more problems than any one person deserved:

- *Spiritual suffering*—He was frustrated spiritually, often felt "overmatched" as a prophet, and had a long-running lover's quarrel with God.

- *Social suffering*—God didn't allow him to marry, attend festive occasions, or mourn the dead.

- *Physical suffering*—Jeremiah was frequently in danger, threatened constantly, and often in prison.

• *Emotional suffering*—Jeremiah told more about his emotional anguish than any other prophet. He was isolated, misunderstood, unpopular, and unhappy.

No wonder the motel business looked good to him! He had no wife, no children, no career, no social life, and no support group. He was stranded on a spiritual, emotional island. To someone like Jeremiah, that little motel in the wilderness would look awfully inviting.

Eventually, he got his opportunity. About twenty years after he first expressed his desire for the wilderness motel, Jeremiah was given the freedom to do whatever he wanted to do. In chapter 40, we read that Jeremiah was bound in chains and being moved to Babylon with other captives. All that he had prophesied had come true, and the people of Judah were being carried off into captivity, just as he had reluctantly predicted.

But when the commander of the guard recognized Jeremiah, he loosed Jeremiah's chains and set him free. He acknowledged that Jeremiah had been right about everything, and then he offered Jeremiah a golden opportunity: "Come with me to Babylon, if you like, and I will look after you; but if you do not want to, then don't come. Look, the whole country lies before you; go wherever you please" (Jer. 40:4).

"Go wherever you please." Don't you know those were sweet words to Jeremiah's ears? Don't you know he had thoughts again of that wilderness motel? Finally, finally, he could get out of the prophet business and into the motel business.

But, surprisingly, he didn't do it. "So Jeremiah went to Gedaliah son of Ahikam at Mizpah and stayed with him among the people who were left behind" (Jer 40:6). You know what Jeremiah did? With this golden opportunity knocking on his door, he shut the door, went to live among the people not transported to Babylon, and kept being a prophet. He kept preaching, being criticized, and feeling alone.

You wonder about that, don't you? Perhaps by then he was "hooked" on a life of isolation and persecution and couldn't feel comfortable being comfortable. We all know how easy it is to become so accustomed to something that we can't change even if we want to.

Jeremiah might have been an old dog who simply didn't want to have to learn a new trick.

But it's possible, even probable, that Jeremiah stayed with those people in Judah and remained a prophet among them because of his commitment—commitment to them and commitment to God. It's more than likely that his desire to be faithful trumped his desire to be a motel-keeper. He went to be a prophet at Mizpah instead of a motel-keeper in Babylon because he was committed to a life of faithfulness. Though he was constantly upset with the people of Judah, they were *his* people, and he loved them. Though he was constantly upset at having to prophesy for God, he felt that, for whatever reason, God had called him to the task.

I think it's fair to say that Jeremiah is one of the most outstanding figures in the entire Old Testament. Given his reluctance and hesitancy to become a prophet, this status is something of a surprise. But his secret was his faithfulness to God and to God's people, a faithfulness that enabled him to put his hand to the plow and never look back.

When Jesus asked his disciples who people thought he was, they said, "Some think you're Jeremiah." It's easy to understand why they might have thought so. Both Jesus and Jeremiah were small-town prophets. Both were born near Jerusalem and had a deep love for the city. Neither did his own writing. Both were opposed by the people of their hometowns. Both, as far as we know, never married. Both told candidly of their struggles. Both were falsely accused and arrested. Both were opposed by the religious leaders of their day. Both confronted social evil.

The one common feature that strikes me most forcefully, though, is this one: both valued faithfulness and stayed true to God and God's people to the very end. Jeremiah and Jesus are both models of tenacity, staying true to their calling whatever the cost.

My hope is that Jeremiah, at the end of his life, finally got some joy. My hope is that one day he looked back on all of his trials and tribulations and said, "It was a good life. I fought a good fight, finished the race, and kept the faith. I'm glad I was true to my calling."

I'd like to think there came a day when Jeremiah knew he had made the right choice, that being a prophet of God was even better than running a wilderness motel.

For Reflection and Discussion

1. Have you ever had to get involved with someone who was on a collision course with disaster? How did it turn out?

2. What is your fantasy "getaway"? Would chasing that fantasy be moving *toward* God or *away* from God?

3. Is there ever a time to "chuck it all" and run away? How do you know when it's time?

4. Why do you think Jeremiah didn't go to Babylon when he had the chance? Have you ever regretted not going somewhere when you had the offer?

5. Can you think of modern-day Jeremiahs who stayed faithful even though it was costly?

THE ROLLER COASTER CLUB

Sing to the Lord! Give praise to the Lord. (Jeremiah 20:13)

Why did I ever come out of the womb to see trouble and to end my days in shame? (Jeremiah 20:18)

I'm thinking about starting a group called the "Roller Coaster Club." Membership is open to anyone who consistently rides an emotional roller coaster. Anyone who can be sky-high one day and scraping bottom the next is eligible. I have a hunch the club will not be lacking for members.

Our patron saint will be none other than Jeremiah, who most definitely rode an emotional roller coaster. In fact, I should give you a word of warning before we look at the next hidden treasure. If you have a seat belt handy, you might want to strap it on. As we move through Jeremiah 20, we're going to be in for a wild emotional ride that can make us downright nauseous. To read Jeremiah 20 is to take a roller coaster ride not for the faint of heart. When I read this passage on a recent Wednesday night at our church, two people came up to me after the service to say that Jeremiah was a classic example of someone afflicted with bi-polar disorder.

So, be forewarned. But if you have the stomach for the trip, zoom along with Jeremiah on his up-and-down ride.

The ride begins with *a word of complaint*. After what you read in the previous chapter, you're probably not surprised. Jeremiah was upset and not afraid to express his displeasure to God:

> O Lord, you deceived me, and I was deceived; you overpowered me and prevailed. I am ridiculed all day long; everyone mocks me. Whenever I speak, I cry out proclaiming violence and destruction. So the word of the Lord brought me reproach all day long. (Jer 20:7-8)

The reason for that complaint can be found in the first few verses of Jeremiah 20. A priest named Pashur had had Jeremiah beaten and thrown in jail, and Jeremiah was furious about it. He proceeded to spew venomous words at Pashur, predicting dire things for him and his family.

Jeremiah was upset for the same reason you and I often get upset: he saw firsthand that life isn't fair. Here he was trying to be faithful to God, trying to declare the word of the Lord, and what did he get for his efforts? A beating and imprisonment. Bad things have descended on a good person, and that is always a perplexing, maddening situation. Especially when *you* happen to be the good person!

But then Jeremiah followed that word of complaint with *a word of conviction*: "But if I say, 'I will not mention him or speak any more in his name,' his word is in my heart like a fire, a fire shut up in my bones. I am weary of holding it in; indeed, I cannot" (Jer 20:9).

Jeremiah had said to himself and maybe to a few other people, "Enough of this God business! I've had it. Here are my ordination papers. I'm through with God and through with being a prophet." The motel business beckoned.

As we saw in the last chapter, though, he couldn't quit. There was a fire in his bones that wouldn't go out. God had done something for him, and in him, that he couldn't ignore. As much as he wanted to walk away from his prophetic calling, he couldn't do it because Someone had hold of him and wouldn't let him go.

Next, Jeremiah spoke *a word of conflict*: "I hear many whispering, 'Terror on every side! Report him! Report him!' All my friends are waiting for me to slip, saying, 'Perhaps he will be deceived; then we will prevail over him and take our revenge on him'" (Jer 20:10).

What Jeremiah needed, of course, was a word of encouragement. He needed support and a little help from his friends, but he didn't have a support group and he didn't have any friends. What he had plenty of, though, were enemies. He heard people whispering behind his back, and he felt alone and persecuted. No one cared. No one understood. It seemed to him that the whole world was against him and that he was fighting these battles all by himself.

Then, just after bemoaning the conflict in his life, he spoke a surprising *word of confidence:*

> But the Lord is with me like a mighty warrior; so my persecutors will stumble and not prevail. They will fail and be thoroughly disgraced; their dishonor will never be forgotten. O Lord Almighty, you who examine the righteous and probe the heart and mind, let me see your vengeance upon them, for to you I have committed my cause. Sing to the Lord! Give praise to the Lord! He rescues the life of the needy from the hands of the wicked. (Jer 20:11-13)

Obviously, Jeremiah was down but not out. In spite of his problems and loneliness, he was confident that God was with him and that God would help him triumph over his enemies. In this part of Jeremiah 20, hope abounds, and Jeremiah sings for joy.

Now you see why some commentators think Jeremiah 20 must be a compilation of sayings from different writers. Surely one man couldn't have been on such a drastic emotional roller coaster. Incredibly, it only gets worse in the rest of the chapter. In verses 11-13, though, Jeremiah expresses confidence. God's in his heaven; all's right with the world.

But suddenly and dramatically his roller coaster plunged into the darkness of despair, and he uttered *a word of cursing:*

> Cursed be the day I was born. May the day my mother bore me not be blessed! Cursed be the man who brought my father the news, who made him very glad, saying, "A child is born to you—a son!" May that man be like the towns the Lord overthrew without pity.

May he hear wailing in the morning, a battle cry at noon. For he did not kill me in the womb, with my mother as my grave, her womb enlarged forever. Why did I ever come out of the womb to see trouble and sorrow and to end my days in shame? (Jer 20:14-18)

You can't get much lower than that, can you? Jeremiah was at the very bottom of the pit of despair with no hope of climbing out. Everyone responsible for his birth got cursed, and doom and gloom were everywhere.

Can you see now why those two people at our church thought Jeremiah must have been suffering from an emotional disorder? What a jolting ride! From complaint to conviction to conflict to confidence to cursing, all in twelve verses in the Bible. It's enough to make even the strongest person a little queasy.

But Jeremiah isn't the only person to have taken such a ride. My guess is that many of us—even those of us who deem ourselves "normal" and "well adjusted"—know something of this roller coaster ride. Our ride might not be quite as jarring as Jeremiah's, but don't we too know of emotional and spiritual mood swings? Don't we too know what it's like to be happy one day and miserable the next? Or close to God one day and shut off from God the next? Or happy with our job one day and desperately flipping through the "help wanted" section the next? Don't we sometimes love the church and sometimes wish we didn't have to go? What's going on here?

What's going on is normal human existence. Normal human existence is a roller coaster ride—more harrowing for some than others, but up and down for everybody. Jeremiah 20 is an extreme example of what it's like to be a human being. If you can't stand roller coasters, you probably can't stand life.

You do wonder, don't you, how Jeremiah made it. How did he survive such a wild ride? As I mentioned in the last chapter, I think the answer is found in his faithfulness and in his conviction that God called him. The secret to Jeremiah's faithfulness can be found in the first chapter of the book: "The word of the Lord came to me, saying, 'Before I formed you in the womb I knew you, before you were born I set you apart; I appointed you as a prophet to the nations'" (Jer 1:5).

Jeremiah survived that tumultuous ride because he knew his life was centered in God. He was known by God, called by God, and secure in his relationship to God. He felt free to be honest—even to complain and curse—because he was so secure in that relationship. He could handle anything because he had a sense of the presence of God in his life.

So can we. We too are known by God, called by God, and secure in our relationship to God, which means we can ride our particular roller coaster with a tenacious faith. We have put our hands to the roller coaster and will never look back. Through all of the ups and downs of the journey, there is a fire somewhere deep down in our bones, a fire that nothing can put out.

For Reflection and Discussion
1. Do you qualify for membership in the Roller Coaster Club? Do you have friends and relatives who could join the club?

2. Have you ever wanted to give up on church and Christianity, but couldn't?

3. Where do you go to find encouragement and support when you're on the roller coaster?

4. Do you think it is normal for Christians to ride the roller coaster?

5. What does it mean to be "centered in God"? How do we learn to sense the presence of God?

A FLICKER
OF FAITH

Yet this I call to mind and therefore I have hope: Because of the Lord's great love we are not consumed, for his compassions never fail. They are new every morning; great is your faithfulness. (Lamentations 3:21-23)

The book of Lamentations is just that—a book of lamentations mourning the capture of Jerusalem by the Babylonians in 587 BC. As such, Lamentations is typically a book we avoid. We like our Bible passages to be uplifting and inspiring, and Lamentations is most definitely not that. It is sad, dark, and depressing. Who wants to go to Bible study or worship and listen to somebody weep? So we flip past Lamentations and hurry on to happier fare.

The traditional view among Bible scholars is that Jeremiah wrote the book of Lamentations, though some scholars say the poetic form of the book and the style of writing make it likely that someone else wrote it. Whoever it was, he had tears in his eyes and a lump in his throat as he wrote. He watched as the city was burned, the temple was desecrated, and his friends and loved ones were hauled off to Babylon. To read the book of Lamentations is to walk a trail of tears, one lament after another, one sob after the next. If you ever get too happy and need to be brought back down to earth, reading Lamentations will likely do the trick.

Why include Lamentations in the Bible at all? Why did the compilers of the canon opt for this book when so many other more inspiring, uplifting books could have been chosen? Aren't the people of God supposed to be singing, happy, and triumphant? Why put a series of dirges in the church's book?

The best reason I can think of is that the compilers of the canon were trying to give an honest portrait of a life with God, and a life with God is not always "positive." A life with God can be filled with grief, doubt, confusion, and anger. If nothing else, the book of Lamentations gives us permission to be honest. When we read these depressing laments, we can breathe a sigh of relief and say, "Thank God, somebody else is not always a victorious Christian."

There is a popular view of Christianity that says we should always be on the mountaintop. In this view, grief, doubt, confusion, and anger are surefire symptoms of faulty faith. The real Christian wakes up singing and keeps on singing whatever may come. But Lamentations is a stark reminder that some in the church's past have not been positive thinkers singing from mountaintops. Some of our spiritual ancestors have tried to be honest and record exactly what they experienced as they took their journey of faith, even if it wasn't upbeat. In their view, happiness plays second fiddle to honesty.

But even in Lamentations, arguably the darkest book in the Bible, there is a flicker of faith. In chapter 3, the writer pauses in the midst of his weeping and wailing and says, "Yet this I call to mind and therefore I have hope" (Lam 3:21). Even in the darkest moments, he tried to remember something that would give him hope. In the entire book of Lamentations, there is only this one brief flicker of faith (3:21-66), and then we're plunged back into the darkness again.

But this one flicker of faith in the third chapter is a jewel. In spite of his desperation and depression (or perhaps *because* of his desperation and depression), the writer came up with a concise strategy for surviving a catastrophe. It's easy to understand and, therefore, accessible to anyone who reads it. For those times when we, too, get desperate and depressed, the flicker of faith in Lamentations is essential reading. It spells out how to survive a catastrophe.

The writer began by remembering *the love of God*: "Because of the Lord's great love we are not consumed, for his compassions never fail" (Lam 3:22). It must have taken a lot of faith to write that as the buildings burned and the people wept all around him. Maybe he didn't even *feel* God's love in that situation. But he declared it nonetheless.

There are times when we have to declare the truth even when we don't *feel* it is true. The writer of Lamentations reminded himself that he was in a covenant with God, that God had promised to love him and his people, and that God would not renege on that promise. The Revised Standard Version translates this verse, "The steadfast love of the Lord never ceases."

Then he remembered *the faithfulness of God*: "They are new every morning; great is your faithfulness. I say to myself, 'The Lord is my portion; therefore I will wait for him'" (Lam 3:23-24). Perhaps the writer was remembering other bleak times in Israel's past, like the bondage in Egypt, when things looked dark. But God hadn't left his people in the darkness forever. In time, all things worked together for good. If God could do that back then, couldn't God do something like that now? If God had proven to be faithful in the past, shouldn't God be trusted to be faithful in the present and future?

Then he remembered that he needed to *wait quietly for God*: "The Lord is good to those whose hope is in him, to the one who seeks him; it is good to wait quietly for the salvation of the Lord" (Lam 3:25-26). Those must have been hard words to write too. The chaos around him called for action. Take up arms against the enemy. Write petitions. Put out fires. Stockpile food. Rally the troops. Dozens of actions could have been taken in that crisis. But the writer remembered to try to still himself, to wait quietly for God, to trust in God's salvation.

That salvation, I think, wasn't just the eventual deliverance from the Babylonians. No, I think the salvation he was writing about was the salvation that could take place *in the midst of* that disaster. God could come and save them, give them hope, rescue them from despair, even while the chaos was going on around them. The Babylonians might capture them, but they could still be *saved*. To remember that, though, they needed to be still. Too much activity would stifle an awareness of God's salvation. So the writer would wait quietly for the salvation of the Lord.

As I said, after this brief flicker of faith, the writer of Lamentations went back into the darkness and once again became a prophet of doom and gloom. The book even ends on a pessimistic note: "Restore us to yourself, O Lord, that we may return; renew our days as of old unless you have utterly rejected us and are angry with us beyond measure" (Lam 5:21-22). That's not exactly a grand finale, is it?

Getting to that finale is not easy, for the book of Lamentations is not an easy read. But an odd, paradoxical realization hits us on the far side of all of that weeping and wailing. We realize that all of the lamenting has actually brightened our spirits! It's the ultimate paradox, but reading Lamentations can make us feel better for two reasons.

First, we feel better because we've been in the presence of honesty. Any time we're in the presence of someone telling the truth, it's a good thing. The writer of Lamentations simply tells the truth about his journey with God. He doesn't try to sell us on God, call us to be more positive, or scold us for not being happier. He simply laments his fate and the fate of his nation and gives us permission to do the same, if we need to do it.

Second, we feel better after reading Lamentations because it reminds us that even on the darkest days, even when everything looks hopeless, it's possible to fashion a personal credo for survival. That's what happens in chapter 3 of the book, and that's what can happen in our catastrophe too. We can stop and try to affirm a few simple truths— "God's love will not leave me," "God will continue to be faithful to me," "I need to be quiet and wait on God in the midst of this crisis"—and hold on to those simple truths like a drowning person holds on to a life preserver.

Jesus once promised that if we have faith even the size of a mustard seed, we will be able to move mountains. It's always amazing what even a little flicker of faith can do.

For Reflection and Discussion

1. Do you agree that a life with God is not always positive? Why or why not?

2. Have you ever formulated a personal plan for surviving a catastrophe? What are the major points in the plan?

3. Has God ever saved you in the midst of your suffering? How did that happen, and how did you know God was there?

4. Lamentations is an honest statement of a person's walk with God. How can we be more honest in our own walk with God?

5. Do you ever worry that you'll lose your faith? What does it mean to have faith the size of a mustard seed?

TO SIT WHERE THEY SIT

I came to the exiles who lived at Tel Abib, near the Kebar River. And there, where they were living, I sat among them for seven days—overwhelmed. (Ezekiel 3:15)

A few chapters back, I said if we took a poll among Christian people and asked them to name the strangest book in the Bible, the Song of Songs would get a large number of votes. I think if we did a poll among Christian people and asked them to name the strangest *character* in the Bible, Ezekiel would be at, or near, the top of the list. Justifiably so. Ezekiel was a bizarre person, definitely hearing music most people never hear.

New Testament scholar Daniel Block wrote,

Not surprisingly, Ezekiel has been the subject of numerous psychoanalytical studies. While prophets were known to act and speak erratically for rhetorical purposes, Ezekiel is in a class of his own. The concentration of so many bizarre features in one individual is without precedent.[1]

Ezekiel had wild dreams and visions. He often acted out his prophecies and became a living "object lesson." He saw images of strange creatures. He once lay bound and naked to prove a point. He dug holes in the walls of houses. That's just the beginning of his weirdness. To say Ezekiel was an eccentric would be like saying Baptists have occasionally disagreed with one another. It would be greatly understating the point.

But, in spite of his eccentricities, Ezekiel gave the people of Judah a new understanding of God. He spoke to them about individual responsibility and told them their future wouldn't be determined by what their forefathers did, but by what *they* did. He gave Judah the first intimations of the concept of the priesthood of the believer when he said God's Spirit wasn't just in the temple but in each person. And he gave them the notion of grace, God's willingness to deal personally with them and to bless them and make them acceptable. His well-known vision of the valley of dry bones made it clear that only God can bring new life to a person or a nation. It's all of God's grace and initiative.

Unlike Jeremiah, Ezekiel actually went to Babylon to deliver his message: "The word of the Lord came to Ezekiel the priest, the son of Buzi, by the Kebar River in the land of the Babylonians. There the hand of the Lord was upon him" (Ezek 1:3). Ezekiel was uprooted from his ministry in Judah and embarked on a ministry in the land of the Babylonians among transient people.

If the people heard him at all, if they did indeed learn the lessons in his weird proclamations, they did so because he had become one of them. He wasn't a prophet from afar, hurling edicts at sinful people from a distance. He was one of them, carried off into captivity just like they were. He began his ministry like this: "I came to the exiles who lived at Tel Abib near the Kebar River. And there, where they were living, I sat among them for seven days—overwhelmed" (Ezek 3:15).

In a world where communication seems to be getting more and more difficult, eccentric Ezekiel has something to teach us. The best way to communicate with people is to go and sit among them, to sit where they sit and be "overwhelmed" by their situation, and then to speak a word from "inside."

That principle is one the church must always remember. Too often our attempts to evangelize come across as attempts to "lob the message from a distance." Eugene Peterson, in his book *Christ Plays in Ten Thousand Places,* wrote,

> Our witness and preaching is commonly detached from a local context that is textured with ongoing personal relationships of responsibility and work. The language is largely formulaic, dominated by the rhetoric of advertising and public relations. This is language suitable for crowds and strangers but of dubious usefulness in conveying anything personal, and Jesus' work of salvation is nothing if not personal.[2]

Effective communication doesn't usually come from *outside* a group, but from *inside.* Effective communication takes place because someone has credibility and has earned the right to speak. Someone speaks not as an outside critic but as an inside supporter. It's always more persuasive to speak from within than from without.

That's why all young preachers should preach their first sermon in their home church. There are three rules for great preaching: (1) Have a sympathetic audience. (2) Have a sympathetic audience. (3) Have a sympathetic audience. When that young preacher stands to deliver the Word for the first time, let it be in that church where they've all watched him grow up, and they love him and want only the best for him.

I had the good sense to preach my first sermon at my home church, the Westview Baptist Church in Houston. I had five pages of notes, and the sermon lasted six minutes. No one taped or recorded sermons back in those days, so, mercifully, there's no record of that sermon. I'm sure it was awful. But the people in my church came by and told me my sermon had absolutely changed their lives. They said mine was one of the finest sermons they had ever heard, that it was packed with profound wisdom.

Why would they lie like that? Why would they be so complimentary of such a poor preacher? Because I was one of them. They had watched me grow up. I was an insider, not an outsider. I had been sitting among them all of my life—at Wednesday night suppers, worship services, and other church events. They *knew* me.

Before he ever uttered a word of condemnation or advice to the exiles in Babylon, Ezekiel went and sat where they sat, was astonished at what he saw and heard, and became one of them. There's an old song that invites us to "walk a mile in my shoes." I guess that's another way of saying what Ezekiel did at the River Kebar. He walked a mile in their shoes.

I used to get irritated at old people who drove their cars too slowly or too dangerously. "They're a menace to society," I'd snarl. I'd shake my head in disgust at them when I saw them on the road. Then one day I rode with my grandmother. My grandfather had died several years earlier, and my grandmother had to drive into Bishop, the little South Texas town where she lived, to get groceries and go to church. She lived out in the country, so she'd drive the few miles into town, and occasionally I'd ride along with her.

What an experience that was! My grandmother had what you could call "a heavy foot." She was like the "little old lady from Pasadena." With her at the wheel, we didn't drive into Bishop. We *flew* into Bishop! To ride with my grandmother was to have your prayer life enhanced.

She told me one time that she didn't really like to drive or want to drive; she merely had no other option. She dreaded getting behind the wheel of her Buick, but she had to if she wanted to get to town. After I rode with her a few times, I couldn't get irritated any longer at old people who drive. They might be like my grandmother, and I started seeing them through completely different eyes.

Wouldn't it make a considerable difference in our marriages, our parenting, and our other relationships if we could hear what Ezekiel heard: "Go and sit among them. Go sit where they sit. Before you criticize, get angry, preach sermons, or even make suggestions, get on the inside and become one of them."

The best example of this kind of communication is not Ezekiel, but Jesus. A preacher named Henry Mitchell once preached a fine sermon from this verse in Ezekiel, and he closed it with this paraphrase of the Parable of the Vineyard and the Wicked Tenant:

In the halls of heaven God the Father called a conference one day to review the progress of communication with the beings on the planet earth; reports were given. There was a report given on the patriarchs, but the report was not good. There was another report given on the judges, but it was not significantly better. There was another report on the kings, and it really was poor. There was a report on the priests and a final report on the prophets, and all of them somehow had failed to communicate.

At the close of the report—the evidence that all had failed—God looked to his right. And before he could ask, his son said, "I'll close the gap; I'll try to reconcile them. I'm going to use a different method. I'm going to go and sit where they sit. And if they sit in temptation, I'll sit in temptation." Somebody said he was tempted in all things like as we. "If they sit in hunger, I'll sit in hunger." And they all record that afterwards he was in hunger from forty days of fasting. "If they sit in thirst, I'll sit in thirst." And on the cross it was that he said, "I thirst." If they sit under a cloud of misunderstanding, I'll sit under a cloud of misunderstanding." And somebody reported that he looked up wistfully one day and said, "Will ye also go away?" "If they sit in sorrow and tears, I'll sit in sorrow and tears." And the shortest verse says that "Jesus wept." If they sit in deep depression, and if they feel abandoned by God himself, I will sit where they sit." And from the cross he cried, "My God, my God, why hast thou forsaken me?"[3]

Jesus gave us the ultimate model for communication. He sat where we sit, and we who would serve him in any capacity should try to do the same.

Notes

[1] Daniel Block, *The Book of Ezekiel*, New International Commentary on the Old Testament (Grand Rapids: Eerdmans, 1997), 10.

[2] Eugene Peterson, *Christ Plays in Ten Thousand Places* (Grand Rapids: Eerdmans, 2005), 217.

[3] Henry Mitchell, *The Recovery of Preaching* (San Francisco: Harper & Row, 1977), 9.

For Reflection and Discussion

1. What does it tell us when God calls someone like Ezekiel to be a prophet?

2. What specific things can you do to "sit with" your spouse, children, friends, and coworkers?

3. Does the church need to work harder at "sitting with" people outside the church? How could we do that?

4. What experiences have you had that enabled you to identify with a person or group you once criticized?

5. Recall some incidents in your own life when people used the "sit where they sit" philosophy to make communication possible.

THE BEST DREAM YOU
COULD EVER HAVE

So he told me and gave me the interpretation of these things: "The four beasts are four kingdoms that will rise from the earth. But the saints of the Most High will receive the kingdom and will possess it forever—yes, for ever and ever." (Daniel 7:16-17)

Someone asked me recently how good I am at interpreting dreams. I had to confess that dream interpretation is not one of my spiritual gifts. In a way, I wish it were, for I have had some strange dreams lately and would like to know what they mean.

The Bible describes a lot of dreams, and those dreams usually turn out to be significant. The biblical writers definitely took dreams seriously. There's even a kind of literature in the Bible that depends primarily on dreams and visions. It's called "apocalyptic literature," and its most obvious example is the book of Revelation. In the apocalyptic books of the Bible, numbers have special meaning, people and events are symbols of other realities, visions are commonplace, and the emphasis is on the end of time.

Daniel is one of those apocalyptic books. It addresses the same historical situation the book of Ezekiel addresses, and, like Ezekiel, Daniel was transported with the exiles to Babylon. The book of Daniel presents us with a magnificent picture of God, a God who is in control of history and who cares for individual people—like Daniel and his three friends, Shadrach, Meshach, and Abednego. The Daniel story reminded those exiles that God would be their God even in Babylon, and it provided them a role model for standing up to the powers that be. Like Daniel, they could triumph in Babylon.

Chapter 7 of the book describes a dream Daniel had. In the dream, four great beasts came out of the sea. The first beast was a lion with the wings of an eagle. The second beast looked like a bear. The third beast looked like a leopard with wings. The fourth beast looked unlike anything Daniel had ever seen. It had large iron teeth and ten horns. It was "terrifying and frightening and very powerful" (Dan 7:7). There also appeared "one like the son of man" who had more power than even these ferocious beasts. He triumphed over them and "was given authority, glory and sovereign power; all peoples, nations and men of every language worshiped him" (Dan 7:14).

Though Daniel was known as a cracker-jack dream interpreter, this one stumped him. He couldn't imagine what those beasts represented and what the dream signified. He began to ask around and finally found someone who could interpret it for him. "So he told me and gave me the interpretation of these things: 'The four great beasts are four kingdoms that will rise from the earth. But the saints of the Most High will receive the kingdom and will possess it forever—yes, for ever and ever'" (Dan 7:17).

The short version of that interpretation goes like this: "At the far end of all your troubles, all will be well. You will receive the kingdom and possess it forever." Imagine how sweet that sounded to the exiles stuck in Babylon. Eventually, these beasts would be overthrown, and they, the saints of the Most High, would dwell in the kingdom of God forever and ever.

Daniel's dream is reminiscent of the dream another exile would have about 700 years later. Exiled on the island of Patmos, John had a different dream, but a dream with the same meaning. He recorded his dream in the book of Revelation. It was a dream of a Holy City coming down out of heaven and a loud voice from the throne declaring that God would now dwell with men. God would be with them forever and wipe away every tear from their eyes. All death, mourning, crying, and pain would be banished, for the old order of things had passed away.

When John had that dream, the early Christians were suffering under the oppressive reign of the Roman Empire. It was a lot like Daniel's time when the people were being persecuted by men and feeling forsaken by God. John's dream did for them exactly what Daniel's dream did for the people in Babylon. It reminded those early Christians of this: at the end of all your troubles, all will be well. You will receive the kingdom and possess it forever.

Both of those dreams transport us to heaven, don't they? Especially the Revelation dream, but even, to some extent, the Daniel dream. They remind us that we, too, can be confident because we know the end of the story. The "son of man" in Daniel's dream did indeed show up, and, as Daniel's dream predicted, "his dominion became an everlasting dominion that would not pass away, and his kingdom became one that would never be destroyed" (Dan 7:14). I sometimes worry that we've lost those dreams and what they signify. The people in Babylon and the people chafing under the boot of the Roman Empire found hope when they remembered the eternal scheme of things. But our culture cares little for tomorrow. Even in the church, we're focused on what our faith can do for us *today*. Songs about heaven seem old-fashioned and out of touch. We speak little of *eternal* life, assuming that everyone is more interested in how to cope with the problems of the *present* life.

When I flip through my sermon files, I notice it's been a while since I've preached a sermon on eternity. Since I'd like my listeners actually to listen when I preach, I'm fixated on the present too. I preach to them about family life, dealing with money, finding peace in a hectic world, coping with grief, and dozens of other "timely" topics. I'm afraid if I put something about heaven in a sermon title that goes on the sign in front of our church, people will stay away in droves. Isn't eternity something they talked about a hundred years ago? Wouldn't that sermon title on the sign make our church look old-fashioned?

But I'm also haunted by something the apostle Paul wrote: "If only for this life we have hope in Christ, we are to be pitied more than all men" (1 Cor 15:19). Something about that rings true for me. If we forget the eternal dimension of faith, we lose something important. If we forget the end of the story, we lose something significant, something that might be more significant than all the "timely" topics we typically focus on in the church today.

Remembering the end of the story enables us to relax, have more joy, and not "sweat" so much in life. Preoccupation with the present makes us uptight and miserable. Focusing only on today makes me think *I'm* responsible, *I* need to do better, *I* need to get my life in order—now!

But focusing on eternity shifts the emphasis to God. God has been working since the beginning of time. God sent Jesus Christ into the world to redeem it. God conquered death and gave us hope. God's got it all together, so why don't I just "cool it" and lean on the Eternal One?

Imagine a group of people sitting around watching a video replay of a football game. You are the only one who actually saw the game live, so you're the only one who knows the final score. You know your team throws a long touchdown pass in the closing seconds of the game to pull off a miracle victory. No one else in the room watching the replay of the game knows what you know. They're nervous and fidgety. Everyone groans when the home team fumbles. Everyone grumbles when the other team intercepts a pass and goes in for a touchdown. But not you. You know the outcome of the game and can enjoy it without anxiety and pressure.

We biblical people know the end of the story: God wins. That's what this dream in Daniel is about. That's what John's dream in Revelation is about. That's what most of the New Testament is about. God scored the winning touchdown at the cross, and the principalities and powers have been defeated once and for all. Now, no matter how menacing the enemy looks, no matter how bad our personal life becomes, we know the end of the story. And we know we win.

I must confess that I have never been particularly moved by the images of heaven in the Bible. Streets of gold and crystal seas don't set my heart aflutter. But when I remember what those images are trying to convey, I get much more excited. What the Bible says is that, at the end of it all, we get to go home. We get to go to a place where there are no tears and no conflict, a place where we are secure in God's eternal love. After wandering homeless for a lifetime, in eternity we finally get to go home.

I remember waking up one morning when I was a teenager and thinking how blessed I was. It was a Saturday morning, so I didn't have to get up and go to school. My mother was frying bacon in the kitchen, and that wonderful aroma wafted into my bedroom. I knew my dad would have a cup of hot tea and the sports page waiting for me on the kitchen table. I lay there, misty-eyed, thinking about how good I had it, thinking I must be the luckiest teenager in the world.

I think that's what heaven will be like. We'll be home at last. And we'll stay misty-eyed most of the time.

Before he died, Jesus called his friends to him and told them they would have some anxiety and trouble after he was gone. But he told them not to worry too much, that he was going to prepare a place for them, that the Father had a big house, and that there would be a room just for them. After the beasts had raged, all would be well, and they would get to go home.

Once you really think about it, that strange dream of Daniel's falls right into line with the rest of the biblical revelation. Once you understand its meaning, it seems more wonderful than strange. It seems like the best dream anyone could have.

For Reflection and Discussion

1. Do you think dreams are significant? How can we learn more from our dreams?

2. Has the church lost its vision of eternity? Does it seem old-fashioned to talk about eternity from the pulpit?

3. What do you think modern people are most concerned about? Does anyone care about eternity anymore?

4. Do the biblical images of heaven excite you? What would be heaven for you?

5. If we forget the end of the story, we lose something significant. What do we lose?

HOW NOT TO
DO RELIGION

Foreigners sap his strength, but he does not realize it. His hair is sprinkled with gray, but he does not notice. Israel's arrogance testifies against him, but despite all this he does not return to the Lord his God or search for him. (Hosea 7:9-10)

Much of the Bible tells us how to live and how to relate to God. But much of the Bible also tells us how *not* to live and how *not* to relate to God. The biblical writers were most forthright in telling us of people who were anything *but* role models.

The prophet Hosea was one of those writers who called people to righteousness by describing *un*righteousness. He did it by using himself as an illustration. Hosea had been jilted by his promiscuous wife, Gomer, and he used that relationship to show how *not* to relate to God.

Just as his wife had been unfaithful to him, Hosea said Israel had been unfaithful to God. But just as he had taken his wife back and loved her in spite of her sin, so God would take back the people of Israel and be true to the covenant with them. One of the key words in the book of Hosea is the Hebrew word *hesed,* which means "loyal love." God's love for Israel would be loyal, in spite of the nation's promiscuity.

In chapter 7 of Hosea, the prophet uses four graphic images to describe the religion of the people of Israel. He says their faith is like *a hot oven, a half-baked cake, a silly dove,* and *a faulty bow.* Those similes give us four pictures of how *not* to relate to God. Hosea 7 presents a handy checklist for how *not* to do religion for every generation.

With regard to personal discipline, Hosea said, the people of Israel were like *a hot oven* (Hos 7:4, 6, 7). It was an image of passion out of control, and he went on to give three examples: their sexual passion, their passion for wine, and their passion for power. These passions were all like a hot oven, burning "like an oven whose fire the baker need not stir."

The ovens Hosea was alluding to were not like our ovens. They were open ovens like our charcoal grills. You didn't cook anything on those ovens until the fire had burned down and the flame had subsided. To try to cook on a hot, flaming oven would be to court disaster. The food might burn. The surroundings might even catch on fire.

It's an image of passions out of control—sex with no boundaries, drinking with no restraint, power with no humility. When you live like a hot oven, your motto is "If it feels good, do it." The people of Israel, according to Hosea, had adopted that as their national credo.

God has always wanted people to have a steadfast focus, to put their hands to the plow and never look back. But in the eighth century BC, God had people with the attention span of a two-year-old. They would chase after any temptation—be it sex, wine, power, or something else—that wandered by. Their fire was out of control, and, Hosea warned, they were about to get burned.

With regard to commitment, Hosea went on to say, the people were *a half-baked cake* (Hos 7:8). Hosea said the people of Israel were like "a flat cake not turned over." In those days, the bakers had to turn a cake to get it done on both sides. We put a cake in our modern ovens and forget about it, but in the eighth century BC, the baker had to be diligent to turn the cake. If she forgot, the cake would get done only on one side.

Hosea used the image of that half-baked cake to describe the commitment of the Israelites. They had "mixed in with other nations," he

said, and lost their distinctiveness. They had a half-baked commitment that made them no different from the godless people around
them. They were Platte River people, a mile wide and an inch deep.
Jimmy Carter once said he was prodded to get serious about his faith
when he heard the question "If you were on trial for being a Christian,
would there be enough evidence to convict you?" Hosea said that for
the people of Israel, the evidence was lacking.

Then Hosea used a third image to depict their sense of direction.
He said it was like *a silly dove* (Hos 7:11). "Easily deceived and sense-
less," he said. It's an image of someone lost, without any sense of
which way to go. The dove might fly this way or that way, but there's
no purpose in any of it. Hosea said the people of Israel would look to
Egypt for help one day and turn to Assyria the next. But the bottom
line was, in their flitting from one allegiance to another, they had
strayed away from God.

I once heard a man described as "having his feet planted firmly in
mid-air." That's what Hosea thought of those people in Israel. Their
feet were planted firmly in mid-air and, like a silly dove, you never
knew where they might land.

Then Hosea said the purpose of the people was like *a faulty bow*
(Hos 7:16). To put that image in more modern terms, those people
were like a gun that wouldn't fire or perhaps a car that wouldn't start.
If they kept doing what they were doing, they wouldn't fulfill their
purpose. They would miss the bull's-eye by a mile.

It might be helpful to recall that the Greek word for "sin" in the
New Testament is *hamartia,* which means "missing the mark." Sin
happens when our lives become like a faulty bow, and all of the arrows
we shoot land far away from the bull's-eye. Our aim gets so out of
whack that we completely lose sight of who God intended us to
become. No one can hit the target with a faulty bow.

Put those four images in Hosea together, and you get a composite
picture of how *not* to do religion. If you have discipline like a hot
oven, commitment like a half-baked cake, a sense of direction like a
silly dove, and a purpose like a faulty bow, you will certainly end up
far, far away from the will of God.

What is especially intriguing (and frightening) about this passage is that the people of Israel evidently didn't see themselves like this at all. They wouldn't have described themselves as hot ovens, half-baked cakes, silly doves, or faulty bows. They thought their faith was fine, thank you, and probably wondered why Hosea was such a naysayer.

But Hosea saw Israel as a foolish man, oblivious to the truth: "Foreigners sap his strength, but he does not realize it. His hair is sprinkled with gray, but he does not notice. Israel's arrogance testifies against him, but despite all this he does not return to the Lord his God or search for him" (Hos 7:9-10). Israel had its head in the sand, ignorant of its spiritual condition. And, according to Hosea, its ignorance was anything but bliss.

Imagine a town that gets its water from a nearby river. The problem is that the river is polluted and poisonous. People in the town keep getting sick and a few even die, but no one knows the river is the cause of it. The townspeople have gotten their water from that river all their lives and see nothing wrong with it. Then someone comes along and tells them the truth. This prophet says, "The entire water system is polluted, and everyone is in danger. You need to start over and get your water from a new river."

That, in a nutshell, is what Hosea was saying. The nation of Israel was polluted. Their whole approach to God was poisonous. Unless they started drawing from a new source, they would continue to get sick and die. But, thank God, there was good water available! It was theirs for the taking if only they would give it a try: "I will heal their waywardness and love them freely, for my anger has turned away from them. I will be like dew to Israel; he will blossom like a lily" (Hos 14:4-5).

If the people of Israel would start drinking this fresh "dew," they would begin to blossom. If they would get on a steady diet of God's water, things would begin to change for the better. Their ovens would become functional and cook to perfection. Their cakes would be done on both sides and taste delicious. Their doves would start flying straight and true. And their bows would begin shooting arrows that hit the bull's-eye of God's will.

The old word for what Hosea wanted those people to do is the word "repent." It's a word with negative connotations in our day, but it's actually one of the most positive words in the dictionary. It means we don't have to keep drinking polluted water. It means we can start drinking from a completely new source, "a spring of water welling up to eternal life" (John 4:14). It means we can turn our lives around and begin to blossom.

For Reflection and Discussion

1. Think of God's "loyal love" to you. How has that love made itself known?

2. Do you think Hosea's four images apply to our culture? How are we like a hot oven, a half-baked cake, a silly dove, and a faulty bow?

3. If you were on trial for being a Christian, would there be enough evidence to convict you?

4. Is it possible that our whole culture is drinking from a polluted river? How do we get a better water supply?

5. Does the word "repent" have negative connotations to you? Recast the word in a positive way, and think about it as God's invitation to find fresh water.

HERALDS OF WHAT WE KNOW

Then the Lord replied: "Write down the revelation and make it plain on tablets so that a herald may run with it. For the revelation awaits an appointed time; it speaks of the end and will not prove false. Though it linger, wait for it; it will certainly come and not delay." (Habakkuk 2:2-3)

A little witnessing button made me miserable for weeks. It was just a lapel button, yellow with a red maze on it. I was supposed to put the button on my shirt and use it to bear witness for Christ. I was probably about sixteen years old at the time, so that meant I'd have to wear the button to high school each day. This was part of a witnessing campaign sponsored by our church. We were all supposed to wear our buttons and, when people asked about them, use that as an open door to give our testimony. The witnessing button was to give us the opportunity to tell people how Jesus had led us out of the maze of life.

My problem was that I didn't want to wear my button. I was shy by nature, and the thought of having to tell people how Jesus had led me out of the maze of life terrified me. So I put the button on my dresser and left it there. But it sneered at me every time I went near it. It called me a coward and quoted the apostle Paul to me: "I am not ashamed of the gospel of Christ." It accused me of not loving Jesus enough even to put a little button on my shirt.

Finally, the button got the best of me. I put it on my shirt one morning as I dressed for school . . . and then put my jacket over it so no one would ever see it! That way I could at least tell the people at church that I had worn my witnessing button.

Do you ever have ambivalent feelings about your witness for Christ? On one hand, you know you are supposed to be "salt" and "light" and that Jesus has commanded you to go into all the world and make disciples. On the other hand, you don't want to be pushy or come across as a religious salesperson hawking the gospel. In other words, you know you should wear that button, but you also want to put a jacket over it.

Perhaps we can find help from the little book of Habakkuk. Habakkuk is another biblical book dealing with the invasion of Judah by the Babylonians. Habakkuk was probably a contemporary of Jeremiah's, and, like Jeremiah, he watched helplessly as invaders ravaged his homeland. Like Lamentations, the book of Habakkuk is a series of laments and complaints. The book was not addressed to the people of Judah, but to God. Habakkuk had serious questions to pose to a God who would let such a catastrophe occur.

Habakkuk's questions centered on three primary concerns:

- God, can you even hear our cries? Are you there at all? Is it foolish to come to you for help? In chapter 1 he cries in exasperation, "How long, O Lord, must I call for help, but you do not listen?" (v. 2).
- God, do you even have the power to change things? Are you impotent? Even if you want to help, do you have the power to do so? Are you really in charge of the world?
- God, do you even care about us? Are you a God who knows us and loves us? If you know us and love us, how could you let such a disaster happen?

Habakkuk had serious questions about God's *hearing*, God's *power*, and God's *love* and brought them boldly before God. By the end of the book of Habakkuk, the prophet had become convinced that God *does* hear, that God *is* in charge of the world, and that God *does* love Judah. He ended the book with an affirmation of faith: Sovereign

Lord is my strength; he makes my feet like the feet of a deer, he enables me to go on the heights" (Hab 3:19).

At one point during his questioning of God, Habakkuk stationed himself on a watchtower to wait for God, to see if God would respond to his cries. Lo and behold, God came: the Lord replied, 'Write down the revelation and make it plain on tablets so that a herald may run with it. For the revelation awaits an appointed time; it speaks of the end and will not prove false. Though it linger, wait for it; it will certainly come and will not delay" (Hab 2:2-3).

Habakkuk wanted to complain and grieve, but God told him to declare what he saw and heard, to write it down and make it plain. God wanted Habakkuk to be a herald of what he experienced, then to pass that word along to another herald who could pass it along to others. Habakkuk might not get all the answers he wanted or all the proof he desired, but he would get something. The revelation would come. It would certainly come and would not delay.

Habakkuk was called to be a witness of what he would see and hear. If you think about it, a witness simply bears witness to what he or she has experienced. When a lawyer puts a witness on the stand, the witness's job is to report the truth, to be honest in telling the story.

Had I remembered that, my witnessing button wouldn't have been so intimidating. I assumed a witness for Jesus had to be more impressive and dramatic than I was. I always admired the apostle Paul's passion and his dramatic conversion experience. Do you think Paul would have been embarrassed to wear a witnessing button? No way! But his story was exciting and full of intrigue. Who wouldn't have wanted to tell that story?

But what if your story is not that dramatic? What if you grew up in a Christian home and became a Christian as a child? What if you never speak in tongues or even *want* to speak in tongues? What if you never hear the audible voice of God? What if you never get miraculously healed or know anyone who did? What if you occasionally have some doubts and wonder if we're all playing a game of wishful thinking? If you have a conversion experience like that, what kind of witness for Jesus can you be?

You can be an honest one. Like Habakkuk, you can be a herald of what you know and have experienced. When you're asked about your witnessing button, you say, "Oh, this is a little button that some of the folks at our church are wearing to remind ourselves of our faith in Christ and to celebrate how he guides us through the maze of life." You don't blow any smoke or try to get too impressive. You just tell the truth in a matter-of-fact way. And your witness has power because it is simple, honest, and real.

When Peter and John were hauled before the Sanhedrin, they said, "We cannot help speaking about what we have seen and heard" (Acts 4:20). That's our simple assignment too, to declare what we have seen and heard. If our journey with God has included Damascus Road experiences, by all means we must tell about them. If we've seen lights, heard voices, and been miraculously rescued from a life of sin, we must tell the world about it.

But if we haven't had those kinds of experiences, we don't need to make them up. We don't have to dress up our testimony to make it more appealing. We simply have to be true to our own experience with God. A good Christian witness simply tells the truth.

That, I think, is what Habakkuk learned when he dialogued with God. He wanted to complain and, in fact, *did* complain. God was not doing enough. There was too much evil in the world. Where was God when the going got tough? Why was God an ever-absent help in a time of trouble? But God interrupted his complaining and said, in essence, "Okay, I'll give you a revelation. Write it down in large letters so that a herald may run with it. You may not get all the answers you want, Habakkuk, but I will give you what you need."

Isn't that true for us too? We long for a fuller revelation of God or a more dramatic experience with God. If God would come out in the open or come to us on a wide-screen in Technicolor, we would be sure of our faith and bold in our witness. Armed with those kinds of experiences, our witness to the world would make Paul's look shy and pitiful by comparison.

Even though we haven't been granted the full revelation we desire, we've been given enough. We've been given a Bible to instruct and encourage us. We've been given the church to be our community of support and worship. We've been given prayer to bolster our spirits. We've been given family and friends who are flesh-and-blood examples of the difference Christ makes in people's lives. We've been given our own experiences with God, quiet and unspectacular though they may be, that enable us to believe. We may not have all of God we *want*. But we have all of God we *need*.

Like Habakkuk, our calling is simply to live and say what we have seen and heard. Like him, we are to be honest heralds of what we know.

For Reflection and Discussion

1. Does the thought of witnessing for Christ make you nervous? If so, how do you handle it?

2. Do you think most Christians are too aggressive or not aggressive enough when it comes to evangelism?

3. Have you ever longed for a more dramatic testimony? Why doesn't God give everyone a Damascus Road experience?

4. If you were to be a herald of what you know and honestly recount your story, what would you say?

5. Do you agree that we might not have been given all we want, but we've been given all we need? What, specifically, have you been given to enable you to be a herald of faith?

UNFINISHED BUSINESS

"The glory of this present house will be greater than the glory of the former house," says the Lord Almighty. "And in this place I will grant peace," declares the Lord Almighty. (Haggai 2:9)

Have you ever been disappointed by something you were looking forward to? Maybe it was a long-awaited trip that turned out to be a fiasco or a big football game that turned out to be a runaway victory for the other team. We've all been there, I'm sure, and can testify that reality often doesn't measure up to expectations.

I once took Sherry to Bishop, Texas, to see my grandparent's place there. Bishop was the site of many of my best childhood memories, and I wanted her to see how great a place it was. I told her about my grandfather's huge cotton gin where I would go to play in the cotton seed and, on certain special nights, to spend the night in a trailer house with my grandfather. I told her about my grandparents' huge house, where we celebrated so many family occasions, the biggest house I had ever seen.

Unbeknownst to me, a miraculous shrinkage had taken place through the years. That huge cotton gin had shrunk into a small, shabby place not at all like the giant place I remembered it to be. That huge mansion with all of those rooms had shrunk into an average-sized house, not much bigger than our house in San Antonio. I tried to explain to Sherry that these places were much larger and more impressive when I was a child, but it was a "tough sell." She wasn't buying my miracle shrinkage story.

Something like that happened to the people of Judah when, after seventy long years in Babylon, they got to go home. Things had changed dramatically. Familiar landmarks had been destroyed. Familiar people had died. It wasn't the wonderland they remembered it to be. The miracle shrinkage phenomenon had done its dastardly work.

Several books in the Bible address this period in the nation's history. Ezra and Nehemiah give the history of the people's return. Haggai, Zechariah, Malachi, and Isaiah 56–66 encourage the returning exiles to be faithful to God as they move back to their homeland and settle in. These people had some unfinished business to attend to, and the prophets of God wanted them to get on with it.

To accomplish this unfinished business, the returning exiles had to do three things. Reclaiming their rightful place was a three-step process, and the prophet Haggai called them to start that process immediately.

First, they had to get over their disappointment that things weren't as they dreamed them to be. When they got back to "home sweet home," they discovered things weren't sweet at all. There was a drought in the land, inflation was high, and jobs were impossible to find. Buildings were in ruins, and fields were empty. Seventy years is a long time to be gone. A lot can change in seventy years. In Haggai 1:9, God candidly sums it up: "You expected much, but see, it turned out to be little." The miraculous shrinking phenomenon in all of its glory!

The crucial first step in accomplishing their unfinished business was for the people not to be overwhelmed by discouragement and disappointment. Isn't that true for everyone? When life unfolds in a different way than we envisioned and we have to settle into some kind of Plan B, the first indispensable step is not to succumb to despair.

Can you imagine how it must have felt to those people finally getting to come back home, anticipating this great homecoming? But nothing exciting happened. There were no parades. No parties. No welcome home banners. Just drought, inflation, barren fields, and a bunch of strangers paying them no mind.

I thought of that time Jesus had his homecoming and went back to Nazareth. He stood up in the synagogue on the Sabbath and taught the Scriptures to the home folks but got something less than a positive response. Mark, in recording the homecoming, said the people in Nazareth "took offense at him" (Mark 6:3). Luke's version of the story is even more dramatic. Luke said the home folks wanted to throw Jesus off a cliff!

So what did Jesus do? How did he handle that rejection on his homecoming day? According to Luke, Jesus didn't mope around and give up on his ministry; he just went down the road to Capernaum, and "the people there were amazed at his teaching, because his message had authority" (Luke 4:32). Jesus moved on down the road to Capernaum and did amazing, wonderful things there.

That was the challenge facing those returning exiles. Could they overcome their disappointment and be faithful to God? Could they move beyond the sadness of that homecoming? Could they find enough faith to defeat their disillusionment?

The second part of the recovery process was renewing their covenant to God. Through the prophet Haggai, God reminded them of the old covenant: "'Be strong all you people of the land,' declares the Lord, 'and work. For I am with you,' declares the Lord Almighty. 'This is what I covenanted with you when you came out of Egypt. And my spirit remains among you. Do not fear'" (Hag 2:4-5).

Remember that old covenant and renew it, God said. Through the prophet Zechariah came a similar invitation: "'Return to me,' declares the Lord Almighty, 'and I will return to you'" (Zech 1:3). The second phase of taking care of the unfinished business was to return to God. Seventy years in exile had taken its toll on their faith. They had some returning and renewing to do.

We sometimes sing an old hymn in worship titled "Come, Thou Fount of Every Blessing," and one verse offers this candid confession: "Prone to wander, Lord, I feel it. Prone to leave the God I love." That old hymn says it for all of us, I suspect. We're all prone to wander. We're all prone to leave the God we love.

Most of the time, that wandering is not intentional. Few people consciously decide to quit on God. Maybe occasionally someone will say, "I've had it. I don't believe this stuff any more. I'm washing my hands of this God business." But usually our wandering is unintentional. We get busy doing a lot of good things and forget the covenant we made with God at some point in the past. God inadvertently gets pushed into the corner of our lives while we focus on a bunch of other priorities.

That means that, like the people of Judah, we have to renew the covenant from time to time. We have to confess that we have been chasing after other gods and choose to let God be God again.

The third, and final, step the people had to take in dealing with unfinished business was to do the specific thing God was calling them to do. In their case, it was rebuilding the temple in Jerusalem. The thought of doing that had to be daunting but exciting. Through Haggai, God offered this encouraging word: "'The glory of this present house will be greater than the glory of the former house,'says the Lord Almighty. 'And in this place I will grant peace,' declares the Lord Almighty" (Hag 2:9).

That was their agenda. Those were their marching orders. They were to rebuild the temple in Jerusalem, assured by God that this second temple would be even more glorious than the first one. In the process, they would be rebuilding their relationship to God. Rebuilding the temple meant more than erecting stones and hammering nails; it meant making God supreme over their lives again. It wasn't just a *physical* project; it was also a *spiritual* project.

What, we think to ourselves when we read about these ancient people, is the one thing God might be calling us to do? What specific thing is our unfinished business? Reconciling with someone from whom we've been estranged? Finishing that book we started a long time ago? Graduating from high school or college? Getting our children raised? Writing the dissertation? Coming to a better understanding of the Bible? What is the one thing we need to do next to be faithful to God?

No doubt that "one thing" is different for each of us. We have different pasts, different goals, different personalities. God calls each of us in different ways to do different things. But however we choose to address our own unfinished business, the process is just like the one those returning exiles had to go through back in 520 BC.

We have to deal with our disappointment and not get derailed by it. We have to keep renewing our covenant with God. And we have to get busy doing the one specific thing we feel God is calling us to do.

For those people returning home after seventy years in exile, it was simple: rebuild the temple. But what about you? What is your unfinished business? What's next on your "to-do" list?

Most importantly, will you do it?

For Reflection and Discussion

1. Can you think of personal examples of "the miracle shrinkage phenomenon"? Describe them.

2. Have you ever had a homecoming experience that fizzled? How did you handle your disappointment?

3. Is it time to renew your covenant with God? Have you wandered away and need to return and renew?

4. What do you sense God is calling you to do at this moment in your life? What are today's marching orders?

5. What is keeping you from tending to your unfinished business?

SHOUTING THE WHISPER

What I tell you in the dark, speak in the daylight; what is whispered in your ear, proclaim from the roofs. (Matthew 10:27)

The first time I remember hearing this verse was in a sermon by Fred Craddock. After hearing the sermon, I asked myself two questions: How can I learn to preach like Craddock? And why haven't I ever heard that verse before? It's a verse I've used often since I heard Craddock preach from it, and it has given me my favorite definition for the word "faith." I want to offer the verse to you as our first hidden treasure from the New Testament.

Before we look at the verse, let me try to put it in context for you. In Matthew 10, Jesus has picked his disciples and is getting ready to send them out on their first assignment. In other words, spring training was over, and it was time to begin the real season. Jesus had handpicked the Twelve, but now it was time for them to begin their ministry. Matthew 10 is a manual of instructions for the Twelve as they move out into the world for the first time as ambassadors of a new kingdom.

Jesus offered them much advice as they began their journey: Go only to the lost sheep of Israel. Travel lightly. If people don't receive you, shake the dust off your feet and move on. Be ready for persecution. Don't be afraid of any man. Remember, you have One who knows and loves you. . . . It was encouraging but candid advice.

Buried in that manual of instruction is the verse I want you to see. "What I tell you in the dark, speak in the daylight; what is whispered in your ear, proclaim from the roofs" (Matt 10:27). The disciples were to take the whispers of God and shout them from the housetop. That verse reminds us of two truths as we, too, move out into the world on assignment for Christ.

First, the word of God is a whisper. "What is whispered in your ear . . . ," Jesus told them. I wish that wasn't true. I wish God shouted. I wish God were more audible and visible. But my own experience matches Jesus' words. If I have heard God at all, it has been in a whisper.

Not long ago, I was driving my little pickup to the church, and a car in front of me caught my attention. It was a black Mercedes, driven by a sophisticated-looking Oriental woman. Her car had large stick-on letters on the back windshield, and the message read, "I saw Jesus in the clouds. He spoke to me and said to tell you he is alive."

I don't know about you, but I'm envious of that woman. I want to see Jesus in the clouds too, have him speak to me, and know for certain he is alive. When I sat in my recliner those many years ago at seminary, waiting for God to come to me, that's the kind of experience I was looking for. But I waited and waited, and God never showed up. There was no voice, no miracle. The phone didn't even ring. Unlike my neighbor in the Mercedes, I never got to see Jesus in the clouds or hear him speak to me.

In retrospect, I see that I was trying to "call the shots" with God. I was trying to tell God how and when the revelation should take place. Now I know better. *God* sets the terms. My part is to be patient and to listen very, very closely.

The word of God is a whisper, Jesus said, and while that's not what we want, it's better than nothing. The good news in that pronouncement is that God *does* communicate with us. If there's one thing the Bible teaches us about God, it's that God is in the revelation business. God *wants* to relate to us.

There's always the temptation to believe God was once in the revelation business, but somewhere around the end of the first century, God's revelation license expired and the communication stopped. It's tempting to believe God was at work back in biblical days, firing up those Old Testament prophets and giving power to people like Peter and Paul. But, at the end of the first century, all of that ended. Now, we Christians have to be content with remembering "the good old days," when God actually communicated with people.

When we succumb to that temptation, our journey with God becomes nothing more than memorizing Bible verses and telling stories of yesterday. We forget that those stories in the Bible are there precisely to remind us that God will always communicate with those who know how to listen.

Does it surprise you to think that God can be as active and alive in you as he was in the people in Bible times? That's the good news in saying that the word of God is a whisper. It acknowledges that God *does* communicate.

But the bad news is that it *is* a whisper, and a whisper is not easy to hear. We can get so distracted and have so much noise in our lives that we couldn't hear a divine shout, much less a divine whisper. To hear a whisper you have to be still and concentrate.

When I was coaching my son's Little League baseball team, I was consistently frustrated by a few of the players who couldn't concentrate on baseball. We had a right fielder who enjoyed picking flowers. Our left fielder and center fielder often had rock fights. I finally coined an acronym to describe their condition. It was BADD: Baseball Attention Deficit Disorder. Often I would have to say to these distracted outfielders, "Hey guys, how are you going to learn baseball if you don't pay attention?"

There's another common condition we could call SADD: Spiritual Attention Deficit Disorder. When we get this condition, we live out the song I mentioned in the last chapter: "Prone to wander, Lord, I feel it. Prone to leave the God I love." We flit from one noisy activity to the next, chasing busyness like our lives depended on it. Then we have the nerve to get mad at God for never saying anything. As if it's God fault that the communication lines are busy.

Writer Annie Dillard once observed, "You do not have to sit alone in the dark. If, however, you want to look at the stars, you will find that darkness is necessary."[1] So, too, we do not have to be still. If, however, we would like to hear the whispers of God, we will find that stillness and silence are necessary.

The word of God, Jesus said, is a whisper. *But we are to take those whispers and shout them from the housetops.* It seems a little strange and even a bit dishonest. Shouting whispers doesn't seem right.

The first big heresy in the church had to do with this issue. The Gnostics believed that what you heard in a whisper you should keep to a whisper. They made the Christian way a private club, reserved for those who knew the secret codes and special rituals. They took the good news of Jesus Christ and said, "Shhh, this is not for everyone. Let's keep the whisper a whisper."

That wasn't the New Testament way. Take the whispers of God and shout them from the housetops, the writers say in one form or another throughout the New Testament. When they said it, and when Jesus said it in Matthew 10, they weren't talking about being verbally loud. They weren't saying to accost people with your private experiences.

They were talking about a private experience that changes your public life. They were saying that those faint whispers of God are what you have to bet your life on and that those faint whispers of God end up having public consequences.

We are to take those whispers and pray as if we believe in God with all of our hearts. We are to take those whispers and minister to "the least of these" as if they are Jesus himself. We are to take those whispers and give our money as if the kingdom of God depends on our generosity. We are to take those whispers and preach Jesus from the pulpit until we run out of breath. To put it simply: we are to take those whispers—those faint, almost inaudible whispers—and become fools for Jesus' sake.

I'm always skeptical when someone comes to me and says, "God told me . . . ." I grimace when I hear these words and usually find that what God has told the person is not at all what God has told me. I'm leery of that kind of faith and even leery of my neighbor in the Mercedes.

But still . . . I've made most of the significant decisions in my life because I thought God whispered them to me. As one of my friends put it, "It's a little hard to be skeptical of someone else's mystical experience once you've had one of your own."

We talk a lot about faith, sing about faith, and preach sermons about faith. We often try to sound impressive and theological when we do. That's why I like this verse so much. It defines faith for me better than any song or sermon I've ever heard.

Faith is having the audacity to take the whispers of God and shout them from the housetop.

Note

1 Annie Dillard, *Teaching a Stone to Talk* (New York: Harper & Row, 1982), 31.

For Reflection and Discussion
1. How do you define "faith?"

2. Why does God seem to speak less today than in biblical days?

3. How does God speak to you?

4. Would you be skeptical of the woman in the Mercedes?

5. How can we shout the whisper in a way that modern people will listen?

THE CULTURE OF
COMPLAINT

To what can I compare this generation? They are like children sitting in the marketplaces and calling out to others: "We played the flute for you, and you did not dance; we sang a dirge, and you did not mourn." (Matthew 11:16-17)

I clipped from *Newsweek* magazine an article about the widespread dissatisfaction many Americans are now feeling. The article described the *angst* many people have these days, in spite of the fact that they're thriving financially.

The article told of a thirty-one-year-old man who lived in Detroit, had a good job with General Motors, and made a hefty salary. He had two cars, including his beloved Alfa Romeo, and was planning a scuba diving trip to Cancun in a few months. But, in spite of his apparent luxurious lifestyle, something was gnawing at him.

"If I didn't know any better, I'd be perfectly happy with what I'm doing," he said. "But it gets to me when I see my peers, people I relate to, people my same age, doing better than I am. You start to feel discontent."[1]

Ponder that a moment: he's young, employed, financially secure, owns two cars, and takes nice vacations. You would think he would be counting his blessings and thanking his lucky stars. But no, he's feeling disappointment and discontent. Others his age are higher up the ladder of success, and he's not happy about it. I guess the moral of that article is that no matter how much we have, we can always find reason to be discontent.

"To what shall I compare this generation?" Jesus asked. He answered his own question by describing an imaginary scene. In this scene, children are playing in the marketplace. They call out to people who pass by, "We played the flute for you, and you did not dance; we sang a dirge, and you did not mourn." In Jesus' imaginary scene, the children couldn't please the marketplace crowd no matter what they did. The flute couldn't make the crowd dance, and the dirge couldn't make the crowd cry. Whatever they tried, the children couldn't get the crowd to respond.

Jesus had something specific in mind when he painted that imaginary scene and went on, in Matthew 11, to make his point. John the Baptist had come among the people "singing a sad song," and the people had not responded to him. John had been austere and demanding, and the people had said he must be possessed by a demon.

Then Jesus had come among them "playing the flute," and the people had not responded to him either. Jesus had come eating, drinking, and telling good news, and the people had called him a glutton, a drunkard, and a friend of tax collectors and sinners.

This is a generation, Jesus was saying, that cannot be happy, that will always find a reason to complain. If you speak of repentance, as John did, they will complain. If you speak of joy and grace, as Jesus did, they will complain too. With this generation, heads, you lose, and tails, you lose.

Several years ago, a writer named Robert Hughes wrote a book titled *The Culture of Complaint,* and I thought of that title when I read these verses. It's a good way of describing what Jesus observed in the people of his day, and, Hughes said, it's a good way to describe our culture as well. We have become "the culture of complaint."

Charles Sykes would agree. Sykes also wrote a book about this less-than-ideal facet of the American character and said our new national anthem has become *the whine.* In *A Nation of Victims,* Sykes asserts that we whine because, like that young man who was discontent in the midst of luxury, we now feel "entitled." We have developed personalities built around entitlement, and the results have been disastrous. Sykes writes,

> If such a personality type could have a single war cry, it might be "I DESERVE. . . ." As a 1986 book by that title declared in a statement of expectation and entitlement, "I deserve love. I deserve to be trusted. I deserve freedom. I deserve friendship. I deserve respect. I deserve sexual pleasure. I deserve happiness." Only forty years earlier those notions would have been dismissed as absurdities. All of these things could, of course, be earned, sometimes at great cost. But they were simply given to no one. Over time, the rules had changed: the notion of what constituted "normal" had been radically revised.[2]

When "normal" becomes "I deserve," people naturally start to be upset. After all, we're not getting all of the "goodies" we deserve. Some people are higher up the ladder than we are. Life is not fair, and we demand our rights. We gripe and grumble. We become a nation of victims and a culture of complaint.

Obviously, we can all find legitimate reasons to complain. Our schools, churches, families, and businesses are far from perfect and need improving. Obviously, some races and sects have been mistreated and have every reason to stand up for their rights. Not all complaining stems from an unhealthy desire for entitlement. Even Jesus complained about the sick religion of his day.

But these verses in Matthew 11 do make us ponder the legitimacy of our complaints, and they do make us consider the possibility that we're just like Jesus' generation. Play a dirge, and we won't like it. Play the flute, and we won't like that either. Whatever you do, we'll be unhappy, because we haven't received all we deserve. Like that young man in Detroit, we'll keep looking around us at people who are doing better than we are, and we'll feel discontent.

If that young man in Detroit and the Matthew 11 verses give us one end of the complaint spectrum, Paul in his letter to the Philippians gives us the other end. Philippians is a veritable manifesto against complaining. After reading Philippians, it's almost impossible to grumble about anything.

Paul was in prison in Rome when he wrote the letter. As far as we know, he didn't have a nice salary and two cars, and he wasn't anticipating a scuba-diving trip to Cancun. He was mistreated, alone, and facing a most uncertain future. But not one grumble came from his prison cell. In fact, he went out of his way *not* to grumble.

See if you detect even a hint of entitlement in his words:

- "Now I want you to know, brothers, that what has happened to me has really served to advance the gospel"(1:12).
- "Do everything without complaining or arguing, so that you may become blameless and pure, children of God without fault in a crooked and depraved generation . . ."(2:14-15).
- "Forgetting what is behind and straining toward what is ahead, I press on toward the goal to win the prize for which God has called me heavenward in Christ Jesus"(3:13-14).
- "Rejoice in the Lord always. I will say it again: Rejoice!"(3:4).
- "I know what it is to be in need, and I know what it is to have plenty. I have learned the secret of being content in any and every situation, whether well fed or hungry, whether living in plenty or in want. I can do everything through him who gives me strength" (4:11-13).

Think of the contrast. Well-paying job plus fancy cars plus great vacation equals discontent. No job plus prison plus possible execution equals contentment. It makes me wonder what Paul would think about our "culture of complaint." What would he say to a generation whose national anthem is *the whine?*

Sadly, there seems to be something in human nature that likes to whine. One of the oldest pieces of writing in existence is a clay tablet discovered in ancient Babylon. It says, "Alas, alas, things are not what they used to be; children no longer obey their parents; everybody wants to write a book, and the signs are multiplying that the world is soon coming to an end." Ours is not the first, and probably not the last, culture of complaint.

The Matthew 11 passage ends with a "zinger" from Jesus: "But wisdom is proved right by her actions" (Matt 11:19). In *The Message*, Eugene Peterson translates Jesus' words, "Opinion polls don't count for much, do they? The proof of the pudding is in the eating."

The people had rejected John the Baptist. The people were rejecting Jesus. They didn't respond to the dirge, and they didn't respond to the flute. What would Jesus do? He didn't consult the opinion polls, and, in spite of persecution, he didn't resort to complaining. He kept preaching, healing, and loving people. He kept doing exactly what God had called him to do. The proof of the pudding was in the eating.

The Gospel writers record seven words Jesus spoke when he was dying on the cross. There was a word of forgiveness, a word of salvation, a word of affection, a word of loneliness, a word of physical need, a word of trust, and a word of triumph.

It is instructive to remember that not one Gospel writer recorded a word of complaint.

Notes

1 Adam Bryant, "They're Rich (And You're Not)," *Newsweek,* 5 July 1999, 37.

2 Charles Sykes, *A Nation of Victims* (New York: St. Martin's Press, 1992), 41.

For Reflection and Discussion

1. Do you agree that ours is a culture of complaint and that our national anthem has become *the whine*?

2. To what do people feel entitled these days?

3. What did our generation do to create a culture of entitlement? How do we move toward becoming a culture of responsibility and gratitude?

4. What would it take for you to be content?

5. How could the apostle Paul possibly be content in a prison cell?

CALLED TO STAY HOME

As Jesus was getting into the boat, the man who had been demon-possessed begged to go with him. Jesus did not let him, but said, "Go home to your family and tell them how much the Lord has done for you, and how he has had mercy on you." (Mark 5:18-19)

I'm not sure there's a stranger, spookier story in the Bible than the one recounted in Mark 5. It's the story of Jesus and his encounter with Legion, the man possessed by a horde of demons. The story has all the elements of a horror tale: a cemetery, evil spirits, a man in chains screaming at the top of his lungs, and demons taking up residence in pigs and falling to their death in a lake. It's a bizarre tale.

The story of Jesus and Legion is fairly familiar to most of us, I assume. Once you've read it, how could you ever forget it? It's the *end* of the story that we typically overlook, and it's the *end* of the story that qualifies this passage as a hidden treasure. Just in case you've forgotten some of the fine points of the passage, let me quickly refresh your memory.

Jesus had just gotten out of a boat when a man who was completely out of control confronted him. We would say today that the man was insane and needed to be sedated and institutionalized. Mark said the man lived in the cemetery, and no one could subdue him.

Night and day the man would cry out and cut himself with stones. He was a man living out of control.

If you've ever felt your own life spinning slightly out of control, you at least have a clue as to the terror Legion must have felt. There are times, no doubt, when all of us have felt somewhat out of control. We've been in the grasp of drugs, alcohol, fear, grief, depression, or some other "demon" that made our life miserable. We felt powerless to do anything about it.

Amazingly, Jesus didn't run from Legion, even though he must have been a frightening sight to behold. I'm almost sure I would have set a new world's record in the 100-meter dash if Legion had come toward me. Or maybe I would have called the mental health authorities. At the very least, I would have told all of my friends not to go anywhere near that cemetery. But Jesus waded right in. Throughout the Gospels, he has the wonderful capacity to "hang with" people even when they're unlovely, troubled, or out of control.

Jesus asked him his name, and the man replied, "My name is Legion, for we are many" (Mark 5:9). What happened next is hard to imagine and even harder to explain. Jesus sent the many demons in Legion into a herd of pigs, which promptly sent the pigs, all 2,000 of them, crashing into a nearby lake. I cannot tell you how or why Jesus did that. I can only report the facts of the story and let you draw your own conclusions.

Then the people of the community went out to investigate, and

> . . . they saw the man who had been possessed by the legion of demons, sitting there, dressed and in his right mind; and they were afraid. Those who had seen it told the people what had happened to the demon-possessed man—and told about the pigs as well. Then the people began to plead with Jesus to leave their region. (Mark 5:15-17)

That, regrettably, is so true of human nature. When they saw this once-crazy man dressed and in his right mind, the people weren't grateful or ecstatic or curious; they were *afraid.* They didn't go to Jesus to plead with him to stick around so he could make more insane people sane; they went to him and asked him to *leave*. Like all of us, I suppose, those people were disturbed and frightened by the unfamiliar, the unexpected, and the unexplained.

But it's the end of that strange encounter that I want you to notice most. How could I have missed the ending of the story all these years? Legion had been healed, and we can only imagine how he felt. His life had been restored to him, and he must have felt gratitude, excitement, hope, and even disbelief. He experienced his own resurrection, and what a story he now had to tell the world.

He went to Jesus and begged to become one of Jesus' traveling companions. "As Jesus was getting into the boat, the man who had been demon-possessed begged to go with him" (Mark 5:18). That wasn't a surprising request. You can even think of logical reasons why it would have been a good idea:

It would have helped *Legion*. He could have been trained and discipled by Jesus and grown in his faith.

It would have helped *people*. Think of the impact Legion could have had out there on the road. He could have been an inspiration to thousands of people as he traveled with Jesus.

It would have helped *Jesus*. Legion would have given Jesus instant credibility. The "resurrection" of Legion would have been a dramatic example of the power Jesus possessed.

But Jesus wouldn't let him become part of the traveling team and told him, "Go home to your family and tell them how much the Lord has done for you, and how he has had mercy on you" (Mark 5:19). We typically think of Jesus calling people to *go*, but Jesus called Legion to *stay*. He was supposed to stay home with his family and tell them how much Jesus had blessed him and how much grace he had received.

The reason we need to notice the end of this story is that it reminds most of us of our own calling. I think most of us get exactly the same call that Legion got. Some people get unusual calls from God and go to the far corners of the world to declare what Jesus has done for them and how much grace they have received. The vast majority of us, though, are called to stay home with our families and do our ministry there.

That doesn't sound exotic, does it? On the road with Jesus, seeing the world, and doing dramatic things is more what we had in mind. When we read of evangelists and missionaries preaching boldly and risking life and limb to further the gospel, we're thrilled and inspired. We read of their exploits and know that God is doing special things with and through them.

But us? Our story seems anything *but* thrilling and inspiring. Cooking breakfast for the family every morning. Getting the kids ready for school. Trudging off to work every day. Teaching the same Sunday school class year after year. Paying the bills month after month. Doing our "daily devotionals" each morning. There's not much glamour in any of that. We "normal" folks look in awe at those people who are *really* called by God and who *really* get to be Jesus' ambassadors. As for us, we're destined to be second-class citizens of the kingdom, holding the horses while the real battle is joined somewhere else.

I want you to know that your ministry to the faces at your table is as important as the ministry of an evangelist who preaches to thousands or a missionary who carries the gospel around the world. Your ministry to your husband or wife is a ministry reserved for you. If you don't love him or her with a special kind of love, no one will. Your ministry to your child is a ministry reserved for you too. No evangelist or missionary will be able to love that child the way you can. You have a ministry to your family and maybe to a neighbor or a coworker. If you don't do that ministry to that particular person, it simply will not get done. You are God's strategic person in that situation.

To put it another way, you have a parish to tend—a parish whose constituents you can count on one hand, perhaps, but a parish nonetheless. It is *your* parish, and *you* are its pastor, and your parishioners will not fully experience the love of God without *you.*

I know you'll never make headlines. I know you'll do your ministry to the thunderous applause of absolutely no one. I know no author will ever do a Christian biography of your life. I know you could be the president of Christians Anonymous.

But I also know the kingdom of God rises and falls on people like you. How well we do our personal, anonymous ministries will determine whether or not the love of Jesus gets injected into society. Most of us are called to do quiet, invisible things that are absolutely indispensable to the work of Jesus in the world.

My guess is that Legion was disappointed when Jesus told him to stay home. He probably envisioned a life on the road with Jesus, a life of excitement, meaning, and accomplishment. Staying home with his family and telling them how much the Lord had done for him and how much grace he had received must have seemed anti-climactic.

He, no doubt, envisioned a "big ministry." But in calling him to stay home and make a difference there, Jesus taught him the essential truth for anyone in Christian service: to really make a difference for Christ in the world, think small.

For Reflection and Discussion

1. Why do *you* think Jesus wouldn't allow Legion to go with him?

2. Have you ever felt out of control? Do you know people whose lives are out of control right now?

3. How do you know when to approach these out-of-control people and when to run from them?

4. Do you ever feel disappointed that God didn't call you to go somewhere to serve in a dramatic way?

5. Where is your personal parish? Who are the specific people you are to serve and love?

CONVERTED TO WHAT?

While Apollos was at Corinth, Paul took the road through the interior and arrived at Ephesus. There he found some disciples and asked them, "Did you receive the Holy Spirit when you believed?" They answered, "No, we have not even heard that there is a Holy Spirit." So Paul asked, "Then what baptism did you receive?" (Acts 19:1-2)

Years ago, I knew a vivacious young woman named Kris. She was attractive, personable, bubbly, and a joy to be around. Kris met a young man who was a ministerial student and became engaged to him. A few months later I saw Kris, and she didn't seem the same. It was as if someone had drained all of the life and personality out of her. The sparkle was gone, the laughter missing. She wore no makeup and her clothes were drab.

"What happened to Kris?" I asked a mutual acquaintance.

"Oh, she got converted," he said.

Then heretical questions flitted through my mind: Converted to what? Converted to lifelessness? Converted to rules that steal your joy? Converted to a faith that stifles your laughter? I actually had the thought cross my mind that maybe Kris was better off *before* her conversion than she was *after* her conversion.

I thought about Kris as I was reading this passage from Acts 19. Paul had come to Ephesus and learned that some people there had been converted. Paul asked the question, "Converted to what? Baptized into what?" He discovered that those converts had been baptized into the way of John the Baptist, so Paul told them about the way of Jesus, and "they were baptized into the name of the Lord Jesus" (Acts 19:5).

Those Ephesians had an incomplete conversion and baptism. They had embraced John's way, a way of rigid repentance, but they knew nothing of Jesus' way, a way of forgiving grace. I think it is fair to assume that the Ephesians were settling into a life of fearful faith. They were serving God with fear and trembling, and they had a legalistic faith in God. But it wasn't the joyful faith Paul had found in the way of Jesus.

The Ephesians, I guess you could say, had been converted to the religion of the elder brother. Like him, they were faithful, stiff, fearful, envious, and lacking in freedom and joy. There was a party going on, but they didn't know they had been invited. It was up to Paul to extend the invitation.

Paul wanted them to move up a notch on the conversion scale. He wanted them to respond to God out of love and gratitude, not fear. They needed to move beyond John the Baptist and get to Jesus. They needed to know of the Holy Spirit who would fill them with some fabulous fruit: love, joy, peace, patience, kindness, goodness, faithfulness, gentleness, and self-control (see Gal 5:22-23).

We don't know exactly what Paul told those people, but my guess is that he addressed the same themes the apostle John addressed in 1 John 4:

> We know that we live in him and he in us, because he has given us of his Spirit. And we have seen and testify that the Father has sent his Son to be the Savior of the world. If anyone acknowledges that Jesus is the son of God, God lives in him and he in God. And so we know and rely on the love God has for us. God is love. Whoever lives in love lives in God, and God in him. In this way, love is made complete among us so that we will have confidence on the day of judgment, because in this world we are like him. There is no fear in love. But perfect love drives out fear, because fear has to do with punishment. The one who fears is not made perfect in love. We love because he first loved us. (1 John 4:13-19)

That, or something like that, must have been what Paul told those Ephesians to complete their conversion. And that, or something like that, is a word we need to hear repeatedly in our own conversion journey. It's all too easy to revert to the way of John the Baptist and lose sight of the way of Jesus.

Karl Olsson, in his book *Come to the Party*, wrote, "It is apparent that there are two kinds of people in the church: those who bring gifts to God in order to secure his blessing and those who adore him because they are already secure in his blessing."[1] There are *unblessed* Christians, stuck in the way of John the Baptist, trying to earn God's love and win God's blessing. And there are *blessed* Christians, frolicking in the way of Jesus, grateful for God's love and secure in God's blessing.

When we remember those Christians in Ephesus, incomplete in their faith, baptized into something less than the freedom and grace of Jesus, we have to ask, "What about me? What have I been converted to? What have I been baptized to? Am I one of the blessed or unblessed?"

If you have become one of the blessed, if you feel a lot of joy in your faith and find gratitude constantly welling up within you, let me offer a word of caution: Our world is no friend to grace. Our world knows of *religion,* where a person tries to please an angry God. But it knows almost nothing of *gospel,* where a person is home free because of something God has already done.

Let me put it even more strongly: contemporary Christianity is no friend to grace either. The contemporary church knows more about religion than gospel too, and the biggest deterrent to your joy will come from *inside* the community of faith. You will often look around you, take notice of the faith of other believers, and see your own faith take a dramatic nosedive.

It's one of the great ironies of faith: believers do far more to discourage us than unbelievers do. I think it's fair to say that most of us have never been dissuaded by drug dealers, pornographers, and child abusers. Their presence in the world has probably pushed us into even more fervent commitment. If anything, these enemies of the gospel have challenged us to be more dedicated to the way of Jesus.

It's the *believers* who have sabotaged our joy and siphoned our fervor. It's our fellow Christians, marching under the banner of Christ and trying to help establish his kingdom, who have wreaked havoc on our faith. The military has coined a term to describe damage done not by the enemy, but by our own army. They call it "friendly fire." It is friendly fire that does most of us Christians in. Saints wound us much more than sinners.

What do you do with Christians who seem to have been converted to silliness and make the way of Jesus an embarrassment to any thinking person? What do you do with Christians who seem to have been converted to legalism and make the way of Jesus a boring memorization of rules? What do you do with Christians who seem to have been converted to a self-righteous haughtiness that condemns the rest of the world? What do you do with Christians who seem to have been converted to fear, anger, and resentment?

I think I know what most of us do with them: we accept them and never say a negative word about them lest we ourselves come across as angry and resentful. But they take a toll on us nonetheless. They gradually wear down our enthusiasm for the way of Jesus and make us wonder if we even want to be part of such a sad, pitiful parade. If this is what Christianity does to people, we think on our more cynical days, include me *out*.

But on our more faith-filled days, we know that these misguided companions on the way of Jesus don't have to set the course *for us*. Friendly fire might give us some superficial wounds, but it doesn't have to be fatal. We can still embrace grace, live with gratitude, bring forth the fruit of the Spirit, and live in the freedom and security of God's love. In a world filled with unblessed Christians, we can still be blessed. We can still remember that the good news really is good!

Every year, we get a Christmas card from Kris and her family. She eventually married that preacher, and they now have two children. I look long and hard at that picture of her family in the Christmas card, and I think I see the sparkle back. I think I see a hint of a giggle in her eyes. I'm hoping she has moved from the baptism of John to the baptism of Jesus.

I'm hoping she has become one of the blessed.

Note

1 Karl Olsson, *Come to the Party* (Waco: Word Books, 1972), 80-81.

For Reflection and Discussion

1. Think about your own spiritual development. Were you more legalistic at the beginning of the journey than you are now?

2. Do you think most Christians are blessed or unblessed? Why?

3. What are the traits of an unblessed Christian? What are the traits of a blessed Christian?

4. Do you agree that the biggest deterrent to our faith comes from "friendly fire"? Give some examples.

5. How can we be discerning of "friendly fire" without becoming judgmental and critical?

THE PERSEVERANCE
PROGRESSION

Not only so, but we also rejoice in our sufferings, because we know that suffering produces perseverance; perseverance, character; and character, hope. And hope does not disappoint us, because God has poured out his love into our hearts by the Holy Spirit, whom he has given us. (Romans 5:3-5)

Those who know me best know I'm not much of a computer guru. When it comes to computers, I operate at about a second-grade level. I know how to send and receive e-mail, do basic word processing, and surf the Internet. Anything more than that is beyond me.

That's why one of my favorite things on the computer is the "refresh" feature. Occasionally, I'll get a message that reads, "This page cannot be displayed." But I click "refresh," and, presto, there's the page. Or sometimes I'll get a page that looks like it has old information on it, so I'll hit "refresh," and the information is updated immediately. I've decided that clicking "refresh" is like squirting WD-40™ on something. When you don't really know what to do, you give it a try.

I wish life had a "refresh" feature. Then when we got tired and discouraged, we could just click "refresh" and be renewed. Or when we experienced grief and couldn't seem to get over it, we could click "refresh" and be healed. Or when we lost a sense of the presence of

God in our lives, we could hit "refresh," and God would be updated immediately. I can think of a lot of uses for the "refresh" feature in life.

Sadly, there isn't one, and that means we have to find other ways of refreshing ourselves. We have to come up with other methods for dealing with discouragement, overcoming grief, and coping with the absence of God. We have to learn how to renew ourselves or, maybe better said, how to put ourselves in a position where God can renew us.

One of the most practical passages in the entire Bible about personal renewal is the one I want us to consider now. It seems to me that the church has never paid enough attention to this text. It is tucked away in the book of Romans and seldom gets quoted or studied. But Romans 5:1-5 is one of those rare gems that is both simple and profound. It clearly tells us how to climb out of the pit of suffering to rediscover hope and the love of God.

It begins, not surprisingly, with suffering. "*We also rejoice in our sufferings,*" Paul said. Since suffering is a universal experience with which we are all acquainted, the passage is addressing everyone.

Suffering happens whenever we experience some kind of death. It could be the death of a loved one, or it could be the death of a dream, the death of a relationship, or the death of a certain phase of our lives. Suffering happens whenever something that is significant to us dies, and those deaths occur all the way through life. Live long enough, and your history will be lined with tombstones. Death is built into life, and everyone is destined to suffer.

But Paul's counsel was to *rejoice* in our sufferings. He said not to fight suffering, fret about it, or feel persecuted because of it. His surprising advice was to embrace suffering because it could take us on a journey to the love of God. It's not so much that we're supposed to deny our feelings and act as if we're happy to be in this awful mess; it's that we're supposed to look beyond our feelings to see that this suffering can take us somewhere positive. Romans 5 is an invitation to trust that *all* things can work together for good.

The next step in the progression is perseverance. Suffering produces perseverance. I've started calling this process of renewal in Romans 5 "the perseverance progression" because perseverance is the indispensable first step in the process. When something significant in our lives dies and we suffer, the necessary first response is to hang on and not despair. Perseverance is the first domino that has to be pushed in this progression, for without it none of the other dominoes can fall.

There's something straightforward and comforting about that. When trouble comes and suffering invades our serenity, we don't have to act pious and wear a fake smile. We don't have to sing for joy and be a model of faith. We don't have to inspire others with "how well we're holding up." We just have to hang on for dear life. We just have to take one more step and get through one more day. If we'll do that, the rest of the progression can unfold in due time.

The next step in the progression is character. Perseverance produces character. As we hang on and don't despair, we gradually change. The pressure of the suffering changes us. The word translated "character" here was used in the first century to describe a metal that had passed through the fire and been purified. Paul was suggesting that our character becomes "sterling" because we've persevered through our suffering.

Most of the change in our character is not a change we choose. It's a change that comes as we respond with perseverance to one of those deaths we have to go through. We get backed into a corner, put into a tomb, and we grow, change, and become aware of resources we never knew existed. All we do, really, is hang on, and our character gets transformed in the process.

The next step in the progression is hope. Character produces hope. I saw a bumper sticker recently that read, "Now that I've lost hope, I feel much better." But the truth is, we can't live without hope. Hope is what gets us out of bed in the morning. It's hope that keeps us moving into the future to claim what is there.

The promise of Romans 5 is that hope is coming. Suffering produces perseverance, which produces character, which produces hope. Hang on long enough and your character gets transformed, and then this transformed character starts to see some hope.

If you think about it, the only difference between Simon Peter and Judas Iscariot was that Judas lost hope. Both had deserted Jesus and failed him miserably, but Simon Peter hung on long enough to let the perseverance progression run its course. He didn't despair, was eventually forgiven by Jesus, and got a new start. Judas despaired and never let the perseverance progression get going. If he had just endured for even a few days, don't you know that Jesus would have forgiven him and given him a new start too? But Judas never made it to hope in the progression.

The final step in the progression is a new awareness of God's love. Hope doesn't disappoint us, Paul said. This is not pie-in-the-sky-by-and-by or mere wishful thinking. Going through this process leads us to a personal awareness of God's love because *"God has poured out his love into our hearts by the Holy Spirit, whom he has given us"* (Rom 5:5). When we get to this point in the perseverance progression, we burst out of the tomb and claim a new life. It might take hours, days, or even years, but there does come a day of resurrection. The progression is complete.

Much to our chagrin, this process isn't like the "refresh" feature on the computer. I wish we could click on "personal renewal" and make it happen, but life doesn't work that way. Finding renewal is a process of suffering and persevering and having our character changed and finding hope and then experiencing resurrection. We have to follow the program, and it can sometimes be agonizingly slow.

But the incredible assertion of the Christian gospel is that we will never experience a death that doesn't eventually have a resurrection behind it. Every tomb will someday be left behind.

"Thanks be to God! He gives us the victory through our Lord Jesus Christ"(1 Cor 15:57).

For Reflection and Discussion

1. Do you agree that "suffering happens whenever we experience some kind of death"? Besides the death of loved ones, what are some other deaths that make us suffer?

2. How do you "refresh" yourself when you get discouraged?

3. How has your character changed through the years? How much has perseverance had to do with the change?

4. Do you think Jesus would have forgiven Judas? Why or why not?

5. Think of a time when you experienced resurrection. Did you move through the steps of the progression? How long did it take?

THE FADING SPLENDOR

We are not like Moses, who would put a veil over his face to keep the Israelites from gazing at it while the radiance was fading away. (2 Corinthians 3:13)

In Exodus 34, we read that when Moses came down from Mount Sinai his face was radiant because he had been in the presence of the Lord. The passage says Moses put a veil over his face so as not to frighten the people. Evidently he shone so brightly that he was a bit scary!

The apostle Paul used that incident as an illustration when he wrote his second letter to the Corinthian church. But Paul added a surprising and fascinating twist to the story. Paul said Moses put the veil over his face "to keep the Israelites from gazing at it while the radiance was fading"(3:13). In Paul's version of the incident, Moses was trying to hide the fact that he was "losing his divine glow." One translation says he put the veil on "so that the Israelites might not see the fading splendor."

I like Paul's version a lot, primarily because it is so true to my own experience and also because it makes Moses a character with whom we can readily identify. He was the leader of the Israelite people, but the glow of his relationship with God was fading, and he didn't want the people to know. So he put a veil over his face to hide the fading splendor.

Who can't identify with that? Especially those of us in leadership positions in the church. One Sunday we're alert, alive, and positively glowing. God seems close, and the work of the ministry is exciting. But another Sunday, the splendor has mysteriously faded, and we go to church lifeless and doubtful. Of course we don't want anyone to know we're not "glowing," so we put a veil over our faces and gamely carry on anyway.

But it's not just church leaders who wear the veil; people in the pew do it too. In her memoir *Leaving Church,* Barbara Brown Taylor wrote about the people in her Episcopal church:

> As enjoyable as it could be to spend a couple of hours on Sunday morning with people who were at their best, it was also possible to see the strain in some of their smiles, the effort it took to present the most positive, most faithful version of the self. Sometimes I could almost read the truth written out above people's heads: "Please don't believe me. This is only a shard of who I really am." The cost of the pretense was the loss of the real human texture underneath, but since we all thought that was what was expected of us, that was what we delivered.[1]

I can think of quite a few biblical characters who experienced the fading splendor:

- Elijah did miraculous, powerful things as the prophet of God, but then the splendor disappeared. He found himself under a broom tree, exhausted and burned out. He was defeated and ready to give up on life.
- Jeremiah, the prophet of God, stood up against great opposition but often felt the presence of God was missing from his life. He spent a good deal of time weeping and complaining.
- Job was faithful and longsuffering in the midst of his woes, but then the splendor faded, and he started wondering if God cared about him at all.
- David was a man after God's own heart and Israel's great king, but then he lost the wonder of it all, and, long before Jesus prayed it on

the cross, he prayed, "My God, my God, why have you forsaken me?"(Ps 22:1).

• John the Baptist was the great forerunner of Jesus who had so much certainty and boldness, but then, languishing in prison, he lost it all. He sent his followers to ask Jesus if he was really the messiah, or should they wait for another.

All of those biblical heroes probably wished for a veil because their spiritual glow was gone. Though they went down in history as spiritual giants, they didn't always feel like it.

Paul didn't always feel like a spiritual giant either. In fact, the point Paul is making in 2 Corinthians 3 is that he refused to try to be more than he really was. Unlike Moses, Paul wasn't going to put a veil over his face. He was going to let the Corinthians see him in all of his unadorned homeliness: "We have this treasure in jars of clay to show that this all-surpassing power is from God and not from us"(2 Cor 4:7). Paul saw himself as an ordinary clay pot but trusted that God liked to use plain pottery.

Do you remember the following marvelous passage from the children's book *The Velveteen Rabbit*? It reminds me of Paul in 2 Corinthians:

"What is REAL?" asked the Rabbit one day, when they were lying side by side. "Does it mean having things that buzz inside you and a stick-out handle?"

"Real isn't how you're made," said the Skin Horse. "It's a thing that happens to you. When a child loves you for a long time, not just to play with, but REALLY loves you, then you become Real."

"Does it hurt?" asked the Rabbit.

"Sometimes," said the Skin Horse, for he was always truthful. "When you are Real you don't mind being hurt."

"Does it happen all at once, like being wound up, or bit by bit?"

"It doesn't happen all at once. You become. It takes a long time—that's why it doesn't often happen to people who break easily or have sharp edges or have to be carefully kept. Generally, by the time you are Real, most of your hair has been loved off, and your eyes drop out and you get loose in the joints and very shabby. But these things don't matter at all because once you are Real, you can't be ugly except to people who don't understand."[2]

By the time Paul wrote 2 Corinthians, he had become REAL. True, he was loose in the joints and very shabby. But those things didn't really matter because once he was REAL, he couldn't be ugly. He could show the Corinthians his true self, confident that his unveiled face would reflect the Lord's glory.

A cartoon showed a princess, garbed in regal clothes, talking to a handsome prince dressed in a brilliant uniform. She looked disgusted, standing with her hands on her hips, and said to him, "I liked you better as a frog."

There is some truth to that cartoon, don't you think? God uses frogs and people with unveiled faces to make a difference for others. Strangely enough, most people *do* like frogs better than princes. In *Come to the Party,* Karl Olsson writes,

> Ordinary people feel more uneasy about saints, martyrs, and heroes than about sinners, traitors, and cowards. It is very trying to have a saint in for dinner, especially a saint working on being more saintly. Our guilt may cause us to raise pedestals for spiritual giants and prayer warriors, but we would rather have them gracing our sanctuaries than invading our houses.[3]

Go figure: sinners make better witnesses than saints. And ordinary, plain faces are more attractive than faces covered with fancy veils.

Most of us don't have the faith to believe that. We believe our ordinary, plain faces are not attractive enough to point anyone toward God. We don't have the faith to believe that God does have an affinity for ordinary clay pots and that our best witness to the world has little to do with memorizing Bible verses and everything to do with being REAL.

For Paul that meant being Paul—bristly, sensitive, angry, warm, loving, grateful, cerebral, and tough as a boot. For you it means being who you are. For me it means being who I am. Taking off the veil means we come at the world honestly. We don't don masks or climb up on stilts. We live with integrity, which means that what we project on the *outside* is truly what we are on the *inside.*

One reminder, though: by the time we become REAL, most of our hair has been loved off, our eyes have dropped out, and we've gotten loose in the joints and a bit shabby.

Being a Christian witness isn't as easy as it sounds.

Notes

1 Barbara Brown Taylor, *Leaving Church* (San Francisco: HarperSanFrancisco, 2006), 148.

2 Margery Williams, *The Velveteen Rabbit* (New York: Doubleday, 1958), 17.

3 Karl Olsson, *Come to the Party* (Waco: Word Books, 1972), 77.

For Reflection and Discussion

1. Can you recognize people who wear veils? How?

2. Do you ever wear a veil to church? Is it a good thing or a bad thing to wear a veil?

3. What are the characteristics of a REAL person?

4. Do you agree that ordinary people gravitate more toward sinners than saints?

5. What does it take for you to recover the splendor?

RUNNING FROM
THE SHADOW

These are a shadow of the things that were to come; the reality, however, is found in Christ. (Colossians 2:17)

The following message was printed on a brochure at a car rental agency in Tokyo: "When passenger of foot heave in sight, tootle the horn. Trumpet him melodiously at first, but if he still obstacles your passage, then tootle him with vigour." We can figure out what that message is supposed to communicate, but it lost something in the translation, didn't it?

More than 2,000 years ago, Jesus came into the world and proposed, even modeled, a new way of coming at life. But that way has suffered greatly in translation. As we humans have tried to interpret his life and teachings, we've lost the essence of who he was and what he taught.

Judging from the New Testament, this translation problem started early in the Christian movement. Most of Paul's letters, for example, attempt to correct early misconceptions in the church. Even before the first century ended, people were having trouble translating Jesus.

That is evident in Paul's letter to the Colossians. Written only thirty years after Jesus' death and resurrection, the letter addresses how some people in that church were mistranslating Jesus and his way. Colossians is about some early detours on the road of Christian faith.

In Colossians 2, Paul first invites those Christians to reflect on their faith and to remember their roots: "So, then, just as you received Christ Jesus as Lord, continue to live in him, rooted and built up in him, strengthened in the faith as you were taught, and overflowing with thankfulness" (Col 2:6-7). They were to "remember where they came from" and be grateful for their heritage.

Then he offered them this warning: "See to it that no one takes you captive through hollow and deceptive philosophy, which depends on human tradition and the basic principles of this world rather than on Christ" (Col 2:8). There were some alluring detours on the road of faith—like Gnosticism and legalism—and Paul wanted the Colossians to avoid them at all costs.

In John Bunyan's *Pilgrim's Progress*, Christian had begun his journey to the Celestial City when he started receiving advice from Mr. Worldly Wiseman. Christian listened to him, heeded his advice, and found himself in all kinds of trouble:

> When Christians unto Carnal Men give ear
> Out of their way they go and pay for it dear
> For Mister Worldly Wiseman can but show
> A saint the way to bondage and woe.

Mr. Worldly Wiseman had evidently slipped into the church at Colossae, and Paul wanted to warn them about him.

Wouldn't it be wonderful if things always worked out the way they're supposed to? We begin our journey with Christ and start moving down the road with him. We learn and grow along the way and become wise, mature saints. No hassle. No pain. No detours.

For most of us, though, that's not the way the journey goes. Mr. Worldly Wiseman is alive and well and whispering enticing offers in our ear. We listen to him and wind up on some dastardly detours that keep us from wisdom and maturity. For most of us on the road with Christ, it's one step forward and two steps back.

The Christians in Colossae were not being assaulted from *outside*; it was an *inside* job. Mr. Worldly Wiseman had joined the church and was whispering his temptations in a Sunday school class. The people who were wreaking havoc on their faith were religious folks who were serious about their faith. The Colossians were having to deal with "friendly fire."

In Colossians 2, Paul pinpoints three detours the Colossians needed to avoid:

Detour One: Try to look and sound very spiritual. Paul evidently saw in some of the Colossians an exaggerated interest in "religion." They were religious people and proud of it! So the warnings came fast and furious: "Do not let anyone judge you by what you eat or drink, or with regard to a religious festival, a New Moon celebration or a Sabbath day"(Col 2:16). "Do not let anyone who delights in false humility and the worship of angels disqualify you for the prize"(Col 2:18). He told them to beware of people "with an appearance of wisdom, their self-imposed worship, their false humility, and their harsh treatment of the body"(Col 2:23).

Jesus said to pray in secret, give money in private, and fast in a way that no one notices. But these folks in Colossae, like the Pharisees, were into public appearances. They were supremely religious people and wanted the whole world to know it. Paul counseled the Christians in Colossae to avoid the detour of public piety.

Detour Two: Make rules and commandments your primary focus. This group that was leading the church astray must have been fixated on rules. Paul's warning was pointed:

> Since you died with Christ to the basic principles of this world, why, as though you still belonged to it, do you submit to its rules: "Do not handle! Do not taste! Do not touch!"? These are all destined to perish with use, because they are based on human commands and teachings. (Col 2:20-22)

Certainly the biblical commandments are vital to us and must be taken seriously, but a journey with God is more than keeping rules. That's the primary truth Jesus wanted the Pharisees to comprehend, but they never did. A relationship with God is a relationship that grows, adds depth to our lives, offers us continual grace, and is filled with enough mystery to leave us always hungering for more. But a checklist approach to God is much easier to understand and follow, and that was a detour some of the Colossians evidently couldn't resist.

Detour Three: Become judgmental and critical of those around you. There is in Paul's counsel to the Colossians the implication that they are under attack. You feel it when you read the passage. "Do not let anyone judge you,"he said. "Do not let anyone disqualify you for the prize." These super-spiritual, rule-oriented people in their midst were also drawing roadmaps for others and then being super-critical when they didn't follow them.

We all have to be discerning and make judgments, but this must have been the critical, dogmatic kind of judging that fractures relationships. When you're out there doing your best, twisting and catapulting though life, and the judge holds up a score of zero, it's more than a little deflating. Judgment without love is always destructive, and Paul saw that as the third detour the Colossians were being invited to take.

When we look at those three detours, we can see why they would be so enticing to the Christians at Colossae. We can see that because they're so enticing to us! People who are super-spiritual, rule-oriented, and dogmatic are still held up as model saints and prime examples of the way of Jesus. Paul, of course, would beg to differ.

In contrast to this approach to faith, Paul invited them to remember Jesus. The theme of the entire letter is the supremacy of Christ, and, in chapter 2, Paul gives those Colossian Christians a mini-lesson in Christology: Jesus is divine (v. 9). Jesus is sufficient (v. 10). Jesus is the initiator of a new covenant (vv. 11-12). Jesus is the great forgiver (vv. 13-14). And Jesus is victorious over the forces of evil (v. 15). In contrast to the super-spiritual, rule-oriented, judgmental people in their midst, the Colossians were encouraged to look to Jesus, the author and finisher of their faith. In looking at who he was and what he did, they would find what they needed to battle "the shadow."

That's what Paul called this super-spiritual, rule-oriented, dogmatic approach to Christianity. It was but a shadow of the real thing, "but the reality is found in Christ"(Col 2:17). Paul encouraged the Colossians to run from "the shadow" as fast as they could—straight into the life and teachings of Jesus. In him, they would find "the real thing."

The sign on the stage read, "The Motionless Man, Make Him Laugh, Win $100." The temptation was irresistible. For three hours, men, women, boys, and girls tried everything. But Bill Fuqua, the Motionless Man, stood perfectly still.

He says he is sometimes mistaken for a mannequin. He discovered his talent when he was fourteen while standing motionless in front of a Christmas tree as a joke. A woman came up to him, touched him, and said, "Oh, for a second there I thought it was a real person." That launched his career.

The question when you see Bill Fuqua, the Motionless Man, is always "real or unreal?"

That's also the question Colossians 2 makes us consider. When it comes to Christian faith, what is real and what is unreal? Paul's answer to the Colossians is timeless. The faith that looks so religious, with its super-spirituality and focus on rules and a critical spirit, is not real at all. It looks real, but it's just a shadow. The real thing is what you see in Christ.

According to Paul, the best thing we can do to stay off those dastardly detours and to run from the shadow is to keep our eyes resolutely riveted on Jesus.

For Reflection and Discussion

1. Which of the three detours is most tempting to you? To the modern church?

2. What are some of the subtle ways we parade our faith before the world?

3. When you look at contemporary Christianity, do you see the shadow? Why or why not?

4. Rules and morals are important, so how do we know when we've crossed the line and fallen prey to legalism?

5. Is it even possible to see that we're in the shadow? Can we see ourselves clearly enough to know our faith is flawed? What can open our eyes?

UNSPOKEN WITNESS

We hear that some among you are idle. They are not busy; they are busy-bodies. Such people we command and urge in the Lord Jesus Christ to settle down and earn the bread they eat. And as for you, brothers, never tire of doing what is right. (2 Thessalonians 3:11-13)

If you've read much of the New Testament, you know that the apostle Paul wore several hats when he wrote his letters.

Sometimes he put on his "mystical hat" and wrote about the mystery of God, the inexplicable oneness a person could have with Christ, and the intrigue of the Holy Spirit.

Sometimes he put on his "theological hat" and gave the early believers heavy theology. Paul was quite a thinker and challenged the first Christians to think too.

Sometimes Paul put on his "practical hat" and wrote about specific details and situations confronting those first believers. Often he addressed specific situations in specific churches and gave specific advice.

It was good that Paul could wear so many hats as a writer because those early Christians needed all of that counsel. They needed to remember the mystical, that God could miraculously intersect with their lives. They needed to remember the theological, to have some kind of doctrinal framework for their lives. And they needed to remember the practical, to hear a word about the nitty-gritty details of their experience.

When Paul wrote this passage in 2 Thessalonians, he was wearing the third hat, the practical one. There was a problem in the Thessalonian church that Paul needed to address. Some of the members of that church had decided to quit working, and Paul's stern counsel was "If a man will not work, he shall not eat"(2 Thess 3:10).

It's possible that these people were super-spiritual types who failed to assume personal responsibility for their lives. That does happen, you know. People have been known to abdicate all personal responsibility under the guise of being spiritual. "I'm just going to rely on God to meet my needs," they say as they nestle into the recliner with a cup of coffee. Maybe that's what was happening in the Thessalonian church. They were trusting God to do something God was trusting *them* to do.

But there's another possibility too. In his first letter to this church, Paul had written convincingly about the Second Coming of Christ. He advised them to be ready at all times, for "the day of the Lord will come like a thief in the night"(1 Thess 5:2). It's possible that some of the Thessalonians read that letter and decided they could just quit working. If Jesus was getting ready to return, why work, make long-range plans, or try to save money? Just stop everything, and get ready to meet Jesus.

For whatever reason, some of those Christians had stopped working, and Paul told the other Christians to stay away from them. He told the idle ones to go back to work, and he used himself as an example. When he was among the Thessalonians, he reminded them, he worked night and day, laboring so that he would not be a burden to any of them. He wanted to be a model for them to follow.

His passionate plea that these people go back to work stemmed from his understanding of unspoken witness. Paul knew what you and I know—that who we are speaks so loudly people can't hear what we say. The only way for the Thessalonian Christians to influence their friends and neighbors for Christ was for them to be people of integrity, working for their bread, living honest, trustworthy lives. So Paul told them "to never tire of doing what was right"(2 Thess 3:13).

This practical passage reminds us that Christian witness is always spoken *and* unspoken. We've been known to forget that.

I grew up with the notion that evangelism is "selling Jesus to people." I was taught that evangelism is learning certain techniques to convince people to invite Jesus into their hearts. In short, I believed evangelism was primarily about salesmanship and marketing. In the words of Virginia Stem Owens, in her book *The Total Image,* "Where the spirit needs nourishing by dreams and visions, we are substituting the junk food of media hype, convinced that if such tactics can sell detergent, they can also sell Jesus."[1] I was taught that Jesus could be sold just like detergent, so I tried hard to become a good salesman.

But any words we speak must come from a life that has been transformed. Speak the words, by all means. But make sure those words come from an unspoken witness of working for our bread, paying our bills, spending time with our children, loving our husband or wife, giving generously to those who are hurting, practicing forgiveness and grace, and feeling gratitude for all we have. A life like that is mundane, practical, and *evangelistic.*

This 2 Thessalonians text reminds us that our witness to the world is unspoken as well as spoken. Our faith is not a belief system to be sold but a way of life to be modeled.

Recently, there was an article in our local newspaper about a twenty-six-year-old woman who donated a kidney to someone she didn't know. It turned out that a two-year-old baby received her kidney, but when she donated it she didn't know who the recipient would be. When I read that article, one big question consumed me: What motivated that young woman to be so generous? What faith system prompted her to be so giving? Whatever that young woman's faith is, it prompted her not merely to talk about sacrifice but to *do* something sacrificial. I was moved by her sacrifice and curious about the faith that prompted it.

Unspoken witness is so persuasive. The Old Testament story of Ruth and Naomi is a perfect example of its power. The most famous line in the story is the one we usually hear at weddings: "Where you go I will go, and where you stay I will stay. Your people will be my people and your God my God" (Ruth 1:16).

Ruth made that commitment to her mother-in-law, Naomi, and if you think about it, it was an evangelistic moment. Your God will be my God. Why? Why would Ruth want her mother-in-law's God? I think it was because she had been with Naomi, seen the way she had handled her grief, and received her kindness day after day. She chose Naomi's God because she had already chosen Naomi. She had been moved, I think, by unspoken witness.

Jim Ellenwood, one of the early leaders in the YMCA, said one of the most influential moments in his life happened one night when he was a young boy. He said his bedroom door was cracked open, and he saw his father come out of the bedroom where there was no heat to be by the fireplace in the living room. He watched as his father knelt beside a chair there in the living room to pray before he went to bed. His father had no idea anyone was watching; he just did this every night. But Jim Ellenwood said that the unspoken witness of his father influenced him more than all of the sermons on faith and prayer he would hear the rest of his life. It was simple, quiet, and *evangelistic.*

A long time ago, a preacher named Horace Bushnell preached a sermon he titled *The Power of Unconscious Influence.* In that sermon, he said every person has a certain influence that emanates from him or her just as surely as a certain fragrance emanates from a rose. Bushnell said it is our unconscious influence that really influences people. The way to be persuasive, he said, is to have an unconscious influence that is authentically loving.

He was talking about the same thing Paul was getting at in his letter to the Thessalonians: the power of unspoken witness. One reason it's so powerful is that it seeks no notice. It's quiet, genuine, indirect . . . and extremely persuasive.

We can only guess how the Thessalonians responded to Paul's advice to go back to work and to shun people who were idle busybodies. Perhaps they bristled and said, "Who is he to meddle in our affairs? Whether we work or not is none of his business. And who we befriend is none of his business either."

But maybe they "got it." Maybe they read his letter and said, "We can't effectively preach and teach the good news of Jesus unless we're responsible people of integrity. Our spoken witness will be in vain unless our unspoken witness undergirds it. Let's get up and get back to work and be agents of good news as we do."

Note

1 Virginia Stem Owens, *The Total Image* (Grand Rapids: Eerdmans, 1980), 11.

For Reflection and Discussion

1. Did you grow up believing that evangelism is "selling Jesus to people"? How do you define "evangelism" now?

2. Can you think of acts of unspoken witness that have moved and changed you? What were they?

3. In a world sick of salesmanship, how can we share the gospel?

4. Do most Christians err on the side of talking *too much* about their faith, or *too little*?

5. How can we determine what is *our* responsibility in the world and what is *God's*?

GROWING
IN GRACE

But grow in the grace and knowledge of our Lord and Savior Jesus Christ. (2 Peter 3:18)

Hang around the church long enough, and eventually the new wears off. Eventually you know the words to the hymns without even opening the hymnal. Eventually you know what the preacher is going to say as soon as you see the Scripture in the bulletin. Eventually you've heard the story of the prodigal son approached from so many angles you can't imagine there being one you *haven't* heard.

Hang around the church long enough, in other words, and your credo becomes "Been there, done that." You speak your credo with a sigh of regret. You long for something fresh and new, but Sunday after Sunday you go home disappointed. Is it possible you will never again hear a new thought at church?

I know that feeling well, and I guess that feeling prompted me to go looking for hidden treasures in the Bible. I wanted to give you something you don't hear all the time. I was hoping that by traversing the blue highways we could bump into something new and unfamiliar to you, something that might make you say, "I've been in church all my life and never heard *that* before."

But it's possible that these hidden treasures haven't excited you much either. It's possible that some of them are not *hidden,* that you've bumped into them before and wonder why I think they would be anything new to you. It's also possible that they haven't struck you as *treasures*. You could be thinking I'm out here traipsing around looking for something novel in the Bible and not finding much of substance.

Whether you've found these passages to be hidden treasures or not, I do want you to know I'm in full sympathy with you if you ever find yourself saying, "Been there, done that." I, too, long for new truths that will stretch my mind and renew my spirit. I, too, get bogged down in sameness and sometimes wonder if I've learned all the truth about God I will ever know.

But this one sentence in 2 Peter helps me whenever I grow disillusioned and start to sing "Is That All There Is?" It's the last verse in the letter, the parting prayer: "But grow in the grace and knowledge of our Lord and Savior Jesus Christ"(2 Pet 3:18). That one sentence holds an idea that has encouraged me on those days when I feel especially stale and stunted. It implies two ways to grow spiritually, when I typically think of only one.

One way to grow spiritually is to grow in *knowledge*. That's what happened when I first learned the basics of the biblical story in Sunday school. That's what happened when I took a course on the book of Revelation in college and got an entirely new perspective on that book. That's what happened when a few of us at seminary gathered around a saintly old man who gave us a new way of looking at the Bible and moved us from law to grace. That's what happened when I found some mind-opening truth in books, truth that changed me and gave me a sense of wonder at the mystery of God.

I'm talking about those "Aha!" moments when a light suddenly comes on in the brain, and we become aware of a new facet of God, life, or self. We humans are built in such a way that we crave *new* thoughts, *new* experiences, and *new* relationships, and when we get them we feel a rush of satisfaction.

What a thrill it is to grow in knowledge. Thank God for those writers, preachers, Bible scholars, philosophers, scientists, novelists, and thinkers who stretch our minds and give us new ideas to ponder.

But I don't get as many of those new ideas as I'd like. Too often, I'm in the "been there, done that" camp, bored by old truth and lulled by routine. In his book *Creative Ministry,* Henri Nouwen says that for many Christians the good news is neither good nor news.[1] I'm sure he's right, and, even if we somehow manage to keep it good, it's still awfully difficult to keep it news.

Hang around the church long enough, and eventually you will greet even the news of Jesus' life, death, and resurrection with a polite yawn. Announcing the good news in church is like announcing that grass is green. It's true, all right—but not exactly headline material.

That's why I think we need to pay attention to the second way we can grow. We can grow in *grace.* Even when we don't learn something new about God, even when the preacher uses the same hackneyed three-point sermon on the prodigal son, even when the Sunday school literature is almost as exciting as the phone book, we can still grow in grace. That realization can rescue us from disillusionment.

The truth is that we don't have to learn something new in every book we read or every sermon we hear. We can start to focus on growing in grace. Growing in knowledge has to do with the *head;* growing in grace has to do with the *heart.* Even when our brains are not particularly stimulated, our hearts can still be molded and transformed. Just because we're not learning something new doesn't mean we can't grow spiritually.

The truth of the matter is that most of us have more than enough knowledge already. Sure, we would like to stumble on that book that gives us one "Aha!" moment after another. Sure, we would like to hear a sermon that leaves us in awe of the preacher's insight and depth. Sure, we would like to have friends who inspire us with their intellect. But, honestly, don't we already know more than we live? Doesn't our knowledge exceed our performance? Isn't it possible that we reach a certain point in life where our prime task has more to do with growing in grace than growing in knowledge?

As much as I crave knowledge, I know the challenge for me right now is to grow in grace. I need to learn "the grace . . . of our Savior and Lord Jesus Christ." I need to experience and live grace as well as preach it.

For example, for years I've prided myself on my knowledge of the Sermon on the Mount. I've spent a lot of time studying the Sermon on the Mount and can outline its major sections from memory. But now I need to do a better job of *living* the Sermon on the Mount. I need to start living it in quiet, practical ways. When it comes to the Sermon on the Mount, I need to move from knowledge to grace.

As another example, I've preached many times about the fruit of the Spirit in Galatians 5. I've even used that text for a whole series of sermons and addressed a different fruit in each sermon: love, joy, peace, patience, kindness, goodness, faithfulness, gentleness, and self-control. It's a nice series, if I do say so myself. But my challenge now is to grow in grace and start showing more of those fruits in my life. When it comes to the fruit of the Spirit, I need to grow in grace.

I've realized that I'm at the point in my life where I need to quit worrying so much about learning new things and start applying the old things I already know. My heart needs to catch up with my head. I need to grow in the grace of Christ and have my heart changed.

There's something about realizing this that enables us to relax. As long as the preacher has to teach us something new every Sunday, the Sunday school teacher has to have some profound insight, or the author has to explore uncharted territory, we're destined to be disappointed. Once we move the focus off of knowledge and onto grace, we can quit criticizing others and get on with the business of letting God remodel our hearts.

Don't misunderstand. I still wish for us sermons filled with wisdom, books that thrill us with new insight, and people who stimulate us to new depths. I hope all of us will still get to grow in knowledge.

But I'm more interested now in the second way to grow. I wish us a life that is full of grace, forgiveness, and joy. Even if we never learn one more new thing about God, may we live up to what we already know. May we laugh more, trust God more, and be more at peace when we die.

May we all grow in the *grace* of the Lord Jesus Christ.

Notes

[1] Henri J. M. Nouwen, *Creative Ministry* (Garden City, NY, 1971), 25.

For Reflection and Discussion

1. When was the last time you had an "Aha!" moment? When was the last time you had one at church?

2. Do you ever get frustrated that nothing new happens at church? Do you yearn for something fresh?

3. Define for yourself where you need to "grow in grace."

4. Do you agree that most of us already know more than we live, that our hearts need to catch up with our heads?

5. What specific things can you do to learn to laugh more, trust God more, and be more at peace when you die?

TWO STYLES OF LEADERSHIP

I wrote to the church, but Diotrephes, who loves to be first, will have nothing to do with us. (3 John 9)

Demetrius is well spoken of by everyone—and even by the truth itself. (3 John 12)

Mrs. Florence was my fourth-grade teacher and one of those people who shaped my life with her love. Mrs. Florence didn't have any children, so she must have decided to "adopt" her students as her own. She went above and beyond the regular stuff teachers do. She invited the class to come early each morning, before school even started, to learn beginner French, and many of us showed up. What little French I know today came from those sessions in the fourth grade. She gave us special lessons on manners too—which fork to use when, how to show courtesy to girls, and how to set a proper table. What few manners I know today came from the fourth grade too.

I always knew I was Mrs. Florence's favorite student. It was almost embarrassing, really, how much she favored me over the other kids. She picked me to be a member of the school fire patrol. She invited Paul Watkins and me to attend a Rice-Army football game with her and her husband. And she always picked me to do special things for her—erase the board, take a message to the office, and so on. It was so obvious that I was the teacher's pet. I looked forward to going to school each day just to see how Mrs. Florence would display her obvious preference for me.

After I grew up and became an adult, I was talking to a woman who was in that fourth-grade class. I confided to her that I was Mrs. Florence's favorite and that I always felt bad that she so obviously liked me better than the other kids in the class. This woman had the gall to say *she* was Mrs. Florence's favorite and *she* felt embarrassed that it was so obvious that *she* was the teacher's pet. I have never talked to a person more mistaken than that woman!

It dawned on me after that conversation that every child in our fourth-grade class thought he or she was Mrs. Florence's favorite. Mrs. Florence was one of those rare teachers who made every child feel special.

But I also need to tell you about Mrs. Allred.

Mrs. Allred was my fifth-grade teacher, and she ruled the class like a tyrant. She had a list of rules that we had to follow religiously, and, if we didn't, the consequences were swift and certain. Mrs. Allred ruled by intimidation. She was a woman in her fifties who never smiled and never seemed to enjoy teaching. Come to think of it, she never seemed to enjoy *anything*. We heard she drove fifty miles into Houston every day to teach our class, and we always attributed her grumpiness to the long drive. For whatever reason, Mrs. Allred was the antithesis to Mrs. Florence. *No one* in that fifth-grade class felt like the teacher's pet.

Little did I know that I was getting an early lesson in leadership styles. Little did I know that I would keep meeting people like Mrs. Florence and Mrs. Allred all my life. Little did I know that one day I would be a leader and have to choose between those two styles myself.

The little book of 3 John is about leadership styles. It was written to a man named Gaius, one of the leaders in an unnamed church. Gaius was in a church dealing with conflict, and John wrote this letter to give him encouragement and advice. The letter is brief—fourteen verses in our Bible—and probably was written on one sheet of papyrus.

That unnamed church evidently was caught in a tussle between competing leadership styles. The Mrs. Allred character was a man named Diotrephes, and the Mrs. Florence character was a man named Demetrius.

Diotrephes had an authoritarian style that was divisive and contentious. He must have been wreaking havoc on that church, and John had nothing good to say about him. Even the brief description John gave of his leadership style tells us much about Diotrephes:

• He had an ego problem. He "loves to be first"(v. 9), John commented, which says it all.
• He was authoritarian. Diotrephes wouldn't submit to others. If anyone disagreed with him, he wouldn't welcome that person at church anymore and would eventually put that person out of the church (v. 10).
• He was critical of others. Diotrephes gossiped maliciously about others in the church and was even upset with John (v. 10).
• He was inhospitable and unfriendly. John's brief description of Diotrephes makes it clear: Diotrephes wasn't the kind of person you would want to have over for dinner. He wouldn't have been fun company around the fireplace.

Put those four characteristics together, and you have a popular leadership style even today. It's the "Diotrephes-Mrs. Allred-Domination School of Leadership," and its rules are consistent in every generation: Lead by intimidation. Have strict rules and enforce them vigorously. Don't tolerate dissent, or even suggestion. Make fear your primary motivator.

Those rules have defined one style of leadership since humans first made an appearance on earth, and they define a style of leadership currently popular in the American culture. Classrooms, offices, churches, and homes are led by people from this school of leadership. Sometimes institutions thrive—at least numerically and financially—under these domineering leaders. But no one receiving this leadership has ever felt like the leader's pet.

The other character in 3 John was Demetrius, who obviously had opted for another leadership style. Demetrius is a symbol for the Mrs.

Florence School of Leadership, and even the brief description of him in the letter tells us a lot:

- He was a good person. Before writing about Demetrius, John wrote to Gaius, "Dear friend, do not imitate what is evil but what is good. Anyone who does what is good is from God. Anyone who does what is evil has not seen God"(v. 11). The implication was clear: Demetrius was good and from God, and Diotrephes . . . well, you get the point. Demetrius was a man to be imitated, a man who went about doing good.
- He had the support of the group. He was "well spoken of by everyone"(v. 12). Leadership is always a two-way street, and Demetrius was already halfway there.
- He was a person of truth. Demetrius was even supported by the truth itself (v. 12). He wasn't just held in high esteem by the people; truth even applauded him. And so did John.

Put those three characteristics together, and you get the "Demetrius-Mrs. Florence-Submission School of Leadership." It too has always been governed by a certain set of rules: Trust the group. Motivate through encouragement. Look for the best in others. Try to create a yeasty, zany, laughter-filled environment where people enjoy themselves. In this school of leadership, the people being led often believe themselves to be the leader's pet.

The person on the hot seat in 3 John was Gaius. Since the letter was addressed specifically to him, it follows that he was the one who would have to help the church choose which kind of leadership it wanted. Gaius must have been a person of considerable influence in that church, and John wanted him to make his preference clearly known.

Now that 3 John has brought the issue to the surface, we know *we're* on the hot seat as well. We have to decide what kind of leadership style we want in our church too. Do we want Diotrephes or Demetrius as our pastor? Which of those two leadership styles do we want our deacons and committees to choose? Do we want a Mrs. Allred church or a Mrs. Florence church?

The decision about leadership styles extends beyond the church too. We have to decide how we're going to treat our spouses, children, and friends. We have to decide what kinds of leaders we'll be at work, what kind of coaches we'll be to our Little League teams, or what kind of chairpersons we'll be at the clubs. Most of us have leadership positions of one kind or another, and we all have to decide what kinds of leaders we'll be.

Third John brings the issue to our attention and reminds us that our options are simple: Diotrephes or Demetrius? Domination or submission? Rigidity or freedom? The choice we make will determine not only our own happiness but, to a great extent, the happiness of the people we lead.

For Reflection and Discussion

1. What kind of leadership did your parents give you? How has that affected your life?

2. What type of leader are you? How has your leadership style changed through the years?

3. How would you describe the leadership of your church? What kind of leadership do you want for your church?

4. Is there ever a place for the "Diotrephes–Mrs. Allred–Domination School of Leadership"? If so, when?

5. What kind of leadership best motivates you?

HIDDEN MANNA AND
A WHITE STONE

*To him who overcomes, I will give some of the hidden manna. I will
also give him a white stone with a new name written on it, known only
to him who receives it. (Revelation 2:17)*

The most misunderstood book in the Bible is the book of Revelation.
It was written not to give all the details about the end of the world but
to give hope to persecuted Christians at the end of the first century.
Those Christians, struggling to keep their faith alive under the oppressive reign of the Roman Empire, needed a word of encouragement.
John, exiled on the island of Patmos, wrote Revelation to give it to
them. Written in a cryptic code so as to prevent censorship from the
Romans, the book was a treasure chest of good news for discouraged
believers.

Revelation was addressed to seven specific churches in Asia Minor
(modern-day Turkey): Ephesus, Smyrna, Pergamum, Thyatira, Sardis,
Philadelphia, and Laodicea. The words addressed to these churches are
printed in red in some Bibles because, John said, they are the words of
Jesus himself.

As we move toward the finish line of our journey through some of
the hidden treasures of the Bible, I want you to notice what Jesus had
to say to the church at Pergamum. It was a word of hope to those
Christians living in a difficult situation, and it will enable us to end
our journey on a high note.

First, a word about the city of Pergamum. It was a city noted for its wealth and fashion, a sophisticated place of learning. Some scholars think the word Pergamum comes from the same root as the word "parchment." This we know: Pergamum had the second largest library in the ancient world, with more than 200,000 volumes on parchment. Pergamum was also known as the site of many pagan temples. Zeus (the chief Greek god), Roma (the goddess of Rome), Aesculapius (the god of healing), and Augustus Caesar (a Roman emperor) all had temples in their honor in Pergamum. To put it succinctly: Pergamum was a cosmopolitan and *pagan* place.

When Jesus addressed those seven churches in Asia Minor, he used a common pattern. He spoke a word of *commendation*, followed by a word of *condemnation*, followed by a word of *counsel*, and ending with a word of *comfort*. To Pergamum, that pattern unfolded like this:

- *Commendation*—The Christians in Pergamum had remained true to Christ in a difficult situation. Even though a man named Antipas had been martyred in Pergamum, these Christians had not renounced their faith. (Rev 2:13)
- *Condemnation*—Some in the church had fallen under the spell of groups that compromised the gospel. The Balaamites and Nicolaitans were groups that, under the guise of religion, led people to sexual infidelity and idol worship. Those groups were trying to get a foothold in Pergamum, and Jesus told the Christians there to shun them. (Rev 2:14-15)
- *Counsel*—They were told to repent, turn from any compromise they had made with the truth of the gospel, and hold firm to Christ. (Rev 2:16)
- *Comfort*—Here was the word of promise to the people of Pergamum: "To him who overcomes, I will give some of the hidden manna. I will also give him a white stone with a new name written on it, known only to him who receives it"(Rev 2:17).

It is this word of comfort I want you to notice, the promise of hidden manna and a white stone. Those symbols would have had special meaning to the people of Pergamum, and, once we understand them, they can have special meaning to us too.

"Hidden manna" is a reference back to the exodus when the people of Israel were grumbling about how bad things were, and God promised to rain down bread from heaven. The bread arrived every morning, just enough for that day. On the sixth day, the people gathered a double portion of the bread, so they wouldn't have to work on the Sabbath. "The people of Israel called the bread manna. It was white like coriander seed and tasted like wafers made with honey"(Exod 16:31). This manna was daily sustenance and a constant reminder of God's care.

When Jesus promised the people of Pergamum "hidden manna," he was promising something extremely precious: provision for each day, strength to face whatever they had to go through. "Hidden manna" would have conjured up memories of the exodus and how God gave daily bread to their grumbling ancestors in the wilderness. They would get that provision too, Jesus was saying. They could count on divine sustenance and refreshment each day.

This promise of hidden manna reminds me of the promise Moses gave to the tribe of Asher in the book of Deuteronomy. Before he died, he offered a word of blessing to each of the twelve tribes of Israel, and to the tribe of Asher he promised, "Your strength will equal your days"(Deut 33:25). What a great promise! You will find enough strength to face the challenges of each day.

Something like that promise to the tribe of Asher is what the Christians in Pergamum would have heard in that promise of hidden manna. Hidden manna meant they would have unseen help each and every day of their lives. Like that servant of Elisha's I alluded to earlier, they would see horses and chariots of fire on their side any time an enemy encircled their lives. Like their forefathers, they would receive manna from God each morning.

The promise of a white stone also would have conjured up an image in their minds. Pergamum was engaged in the mining of white stone. These people knew all about white stone and how it was used in their culture.

According to William Barclay, there were two common uses for white stone that probably explain this reference in Revelation 2. A person on trial who was acquitted of a crime was given a white stone as a symbol of innocence. A white stone, then, became a symbol for freedom. Show your white stone, and everyone knew you had been set free.

But white stones were also used as prizes. The winner of a race or contest was often given a white stone as a trophy. A soldier returning from victory on the battlefield was often given a white stone in honor of his achievement. A white stone became a symbol of triumph.

So, to the people of Pergamum, the white stone symbolized freedom and victory. The white stone would have reminded them, "It is for freedom that Christ has set us free. Stand firm, then, and do not let yourselves be burdened again by a yoke of slavery" (Gal 5:1). The white stone also would have said to them, "Thanks be to God! He gives us the victory through our Lord Jesus Christ"(1 Cor 15:57).

This white stone, Jesus said, has a name on it, a name only the recipient knows. When you get the white stone, you're the only one who can read what's on it. It happens in the privacy of your own experience with God. Its message is for you alone.

Reading that stone is the most important thing you will ever do. That stone tells you your real name. That stone tells you your personal calling. That stone gives you your truest, and best, identity. Whatever else you do, you must decipher that white stone.

For some time now, we've been chasing all over the pages of Scripture looking for hidden treasures. We've visited Abraham, Bezalel, Micah, Ahimaaz, Naboth, Job, the sons of Korah, Jeremiah, Jesus, Paul, Peter, John, and more. We've paid a call on some books of the Bible we typically ignore—Judges, Song of Songs, Lamentations, Hosea, Habakkuk, Haggai, 2 Thessalonians, 2 Peter, and 3 John. And even when we've visited familiar books in the Bible, we've explored nooks and crannies off the beaten path. I've enjoyed the trip immensely and hope you have too.

But mostly I hope you've caught the strains of a melody that runs throughout Scripture. As we've traveled the back roads of the Bible, I hope you've noticed a theme that winds through most of these hidden treasures, a theme that ties them all together. It's a theme captured well in Jesus' promise to the people of Pergamum: people who know and love God receive hidden manna and a white stone.

The apostle Paul put that theme in one powerful question: "If God is for us, who can be against us?" (Rom 8:31). That's Paul's version of hidden manna and a white stone. If the God of the universe was on his side—loving him, guiding him, forgiving him, empowering him—what did he have to fear? What could possibly defeat him if he had hidden manna and a white stone?

That's why those Israelites erected those stones at Gilgal and why the sons of Korah were filled with wonder. That's why that woman in the Song of Songs was so smitten with her Lover and what the prophet in Isaiah 60 wanted the downtrodden people of Judah to see. That's what kept Jeremiah faithful through all of his troubles and what caused that brief flicker of faith in the dark book of Lamentations. That's the water Hosea wanted the people to taste, and it's the meaning of Daniel's strange dream. That's what we shout from the housetops and the reason we can't join the culture of complaint. That's what gives us hope to go through the perseverance progression, and it's the reason we're filled with joy in a joyless world. God is *for* us, so who or what can possibly be against us?

That's the treasure hidden throughout the pages of Scriptures. We've been given hidden manna and a white stone. Possessing those two gifts, we can face every day with confidence.

I close with the final words in the Bible: "The grace of the Lord Jesus be with God's people. Amen"(Rev 22:21).

For Reflection and Discussion

1. What would be the message Jesus would give to your church?

2. What form does "hidden manna" usually take for you?

3. Why do you think only you can read what is on your white stone? Have you deciphered the message on the stone?

4. Have there been times when you received the "hidden manna" and "a white stone" from God? How and when did they come?

5. Do you agree that there is a melody throughout the Bible promising strength, freedom, and victory to the people of God? What other passages can you remember?

BY WAY OF THANKS...

"No man is an island," John Donne said, and certainly no writer is either. I need to thank a few people for helping me write this book.

Thank you, Woodland Baptist Church, for granting me a sabbatical so that I could have uninterrupted time to write. What a gracious gift that sabbatical was! I am privileged to be your pastor.

Thank you, Chet and Carolyn Rawie, for allowing Sherry and me to invade your space in Oregon and for being the ideal hosts while we were there. We truly settled into paradise there in Alsea and hope to do it again some day.

Thank you, Sherry, for sharing the sabbatical with me, for reading the manuscript and making suggestions, and for helping with the questions at the end of each chapter. The book is better because of you.

Thank you, Eugene Peterson, Fred Craddock, Barbara Brown Taylor, Robert Capon, John Claypool, Howard Butt, and a host of other preachers and writers for giving me many of these hidden treasures. I've claimed them as my own, but some of them rightfully belong to you.

Finally, thank you, readers, for taking the journey with me. A book is useless unless someone reads it. Thank you for traveling the back roads of the Bible with me.